Christopher J. Freet is pastor of Millersville Brethren in Christ Church, Millersville, PA. He has Master of Arts in Religion degrees from Evangelical Seminary in Myerstown, PA, with concentrations in New Testament and World Christianity. He is married to Stacey L. Freet and they have two children.

The *Areopagus Critical Christian Issues* series examines important issues in understanding Christian beliefs and developing sound Christian practice. Each booklet is short — less than 80 pages in length — and provides an academically sound and biblically rooted examination of a particular question about doctrine or practice or an area of basic Christian belief. It is jointly edited by Dr. Allan R. Bevere and Dr. David Alan Black.

A

textualize hospitality in the wake of our flawed perspectives—and thereby recover our missional identity.

Christopher's call resonates with booming clarity. I have witnessed firsthand how absolutely essential hospitality is for missional momentum. In ministries of every size and locale, hospitality proves pivotal in expanding relationships and accomplishing the *missio Dei*.

Courageously read and enjoy Freet's careful work! But watch out. You'll start opening your home, rethinking church, and leading others toward familial authenticity, greater trust, and stronger fulfillment of God's adventuresome mission.

Dr. John Elton Pletcher
Lead pastor, Manor Church, Lancaster, PA
Adjunct faculty, Eastern University and Evangelical Seminary
author of *Henry's Glory: A Story for Discovering Lasting Significance in Your Daily Work*

In my opinion, Chris has written a book that should be read by many believers. As I read his book, I recalled how important hospitality was on each of my trips to Ethiopia, India, and western Africa. I can truly say hospitality helped "me a foreigner" not feel so foreign in the strange land. Two thoughts kept reoccurring to me as I read the book. First, my soul was stirred to have someone in my home. I not only want to be more hospitable. I want my hospitality to be with love and administered in faith. Second, I thought, 'Facetime over Facebook!' Somehow the church in America needs to re-look at hospitality, and Chris's book surely will help many of us take a closer look at "hospitality as a key to missions."

Dr. Jason Evans
Pastor, Bethel Hill Baptist Church, VA

This book is a win-win read. It educates on Bruce Bennett's remarkable system of church planting in the Majority World as part of the Church Multiplication Movement (CMM). In the process of examining the role that hospitality and 'the person of peace' play in it against the practice of hospitality in the Bible, Chris Freet introduces a yet more remarkable notion—that hospitality originates with God. It is part of His own nature. And the Garden of Eden is proof! God is the Host who creates a great abundance for Adam and Eve, His guests. This, as Chris shows, appears then as a leading motif throughout the Bible and the pattern on how the church in the West can and should make God visible to the world through similar acts of hospitality. There is enough in these pages about God, the Church, and Christian Mission to make it a rich source book for the scholar, pastor, and missionary—and for any follower of Christ who wants to invite the stranger in for a really good meal.

H. Douglas Buckwalter
New Testament Professor
Evangelical Seminary Myerstown, PA

In our increasingly multi-cultural world, Chris Freet reminds us of the profound role of hospitality in the encounter with an unbelieving world. Utilizing a careful scriptural study, the author presents an understanding of hospitality that moves beyond a simple welcoming attitude and into an intentional and mutually beneficial encounter with those who differ from us. His works demonstrates unique insights into the role of an unbelieving "person of peace" as gatekeeper for a culture's receptivity of the Gospel—a gatekeeper who can be most effectively encountered through "abundant hospitality." Freet's timely reminder of early Christianity's spiritual practice of hospitality could not come at a better time—when our encounter with "the other" is too often based in ideological dialogue rather than the kind of hospitality that brings our lifestyles into genuine contact with one another.

James E. Ehrman
Affiliate Professor of World Christianity
Evangelical Seminary, Myerstown, PA

A New Look at Hospitality as a Key to Missions

Christopher J. Freet

Energion Publications
Gonzalez, Florida
2014

Scripture quotations are taken from THE HOLY BIBLE, NEW INTERNATIONAL VERSION®, NIV® Copyright © 1973, 1978, 1984, 2011 by Biblica, Inc.® Used by permission. All rights reserved worldwide.

ISBN10: 1-63199-095-0
ISBN13: 978-1-63199-095-3
Library of Congress Control Number: 2014955838

Energion Publications
P. O. Box 841
Gonzalez, FL 32560]

energion.com
pubs@energion.com

TABLE OF CONTENTS

DEDICATION

To my beautiful bride, Stacey, and my amazing daughters,
Emma and Ana.
I thank our Lord daily for the three of you.

ACKNOWLEDGMENTS

This book originated as a thesis for an M.A.R. in World Christianity from Evangelical Seminary. When I first began this project my prayer was that this work would be useful and practical for churches and ministry leaders. At that time I never expected that it would be published as a book. May all the glory go to Jesus Christ.

Since its inception the project has been through many hands, examined by many sets of eyes, and has been formed through much feedback. I am deeply indebted to everyone who has been a part of the process. Writing is truly a group effort and it is a world through which I am still learning how to maneuver.

First, I would like to thank Henry Neufeld and Energion Publications for taking a chance on a virtual unknown and agreeing to publish this work. I am grateful for Henry's vision and the mission of Energion Publications. Also, I am indebted to the editors of the Areopagus Critical Christian Issues series, Allan R. Bevere and David Alan Black, for accepting this manuscript for publication. I am blessed and humbled to be included in such a quality series.

I would also like to acknowledge the faculty at Evangelical Seminary in Myerstown, Pennsylvania. My time learning, as well as being challenged, there has proven to be foundational and formative for my life and ministry. Particularly, I would like to thank Dr. H. Douglas Buckwalter for your guidance and encouragement over the years and especially with this project. Also, Professor James Ehrman has been an integral part of the journey. The guidance and suggestions from these men proved invaluable.

Kristine Frey is someone who helped with the formatting for this project. I am grateful for her time, energy and expertise which helped move this project along.

Finally, I would like to acknowledge my wife, Stacey, and my daughters, Emma and Ana. Thank you for your encouragement and your prayers over the years. I am blessed to share this journey with each of you.

To everyone involved with this project:

"I thank my God every time I remember you."
– Philippians 1:3

August 2014

CHAPTER 1:

INTRODUCTION

Within American culture the role of hospitality appears to have shifted. Where once people depended on the hospitality of others, the role of hospitality has now been handed over to a hospitality industry. Now a person can obtain a college degree in hospitality which entails learning hotel and restaurant management. Rather than seeking room and board with an unknown host for a night or two, people check in at a Holiday Inn, which has a free continental breakfast. Instead of sharing table fellowship with strangers, the stranger intentionally sits at the uncomfortable hard-plastic table and chairs at the local fast-food establishment which is designed to move "consumers" in and out as fast as possible. Now inviting friends over for a shared meal and maybe even some entertainment is deemed hospitality. What happened to the stranger? Taking in the stranger has become even more strange according to an American worldview, thus keeping the stranger on the fringe of society. In this scenario America is potentially missing out on encountering God in the stranger, a concept that, as we will see, permeates the Scriptures.

GOD AS SOURCE

We will begin with God himself. Hospitality is rooted in the Trinity. "Acts of hospitality," writes Christine Pohl, "participate in and reflect God's greater hospitality and therefore hold some connection to the divine, to holy ground" (*Making Room*, p. 13). Expounding on this further, Christine Pohl and Christopher Heuertz write, "Behind the emphasis on friendship and community in mission stands the experience of our relationship with God. Knowing God as one who desires and offers friendship with us powerfully expands our understanding of God as Creator, Judge, Redeemer and Lover of our souls" (*Friendship at the Margins*, p. 29). The offer of hospitality in the biblical sense is deeply rooted in the hospitality of God. Relationship with God through Christ is foundational for all deep and lasting relationships. Without a proper understanding and implementation of this aspect, there can be no hospitality or even friendship in its fullest extent.

DEFINING HOSPITALITY

How much do Americans comprehend what hospitality entails? What patterns of hospitality should Americans examine and emulate? Regarding this concern, Amy Oden remarks:

> No one standard model [of hospitality] prevails, but several practices occur frequently in these texts [from early church history]. Most behaviors fall into the following list: a warm greeting or welcome, visiting, foot washing or bathing, praying, feeding or feasting, lodging, protection, medical care, almsgiving, and sending forth with supplies and/or escort for the journey. We can see in these practices a pattern. Hospitality moves through several stages. It frequently begins with welcome, then turns to restoration of the guest, followed by being with or dwelling with the other, and ends in the sending forth (*And You Welcomed Me*, p. 145).

Biblical hospitality involves welcoming strangers—the "other." Within the pages of the New Testament this action is encompassed in the *philoxenos/philoxenia* word group. We will explore these usages below. Interestingly, pertaining to hospitality in the Old Testament, there are no words that translate to hospitality. Even in the Septuagint the *philoxenos/philoxenia* word group is nowhere to be found. In her book *And You Welcomed Me* (p. 146), Amy Oden provides a paradigm portraying hospitality as a process with several stages. This paradigm will act as a guide for our study. Initially, the other as a guest is invited into the presence of the host through the welcome or greeting. As Oden observes, this initiatory step involves receiving the guest, usually with an offer to serve in some capacity. The next step involves restoring the guest in some form or fashion. Most often, this entails meeting the immediate needs of the guest. Oden describes the next stage of hospitality as the "common life together." It may include lodging the guest or sharing table fellowship. This stage usually brings with it some sort of "reframing" for the parties involved. The final component, then, is the sending forth. This involves letting go or releasing the guest. One important aspect of hospitality involves the issue of dependency. Oden notes, "This stage suggests that hospitality does not create systems of dependence but empowers the other to move on" (p. 147). To illustrate this point, Oden refers to an example offered by the *Didache* 12:2-3: "If it is a traveler who arrives, help him all you can. But he must not stay with you more than two days, or, if necessary, three. If he wants to settle with you and is an artisan, he must work for his living" (p. 148). Accordingly, the goal or outcome of hospitality is centered around improving the interests and situation of the other without creating a dependency on the host in the process.

HOSPITALITY AND OUR GLOBAL CONTEXT

Before moving on, one key issue concerning the American church and the role of hospitality involves the role of migration, immigration and refugees. Today, most nations face issues related to globalization. The world is becoming smaller and smaller. A person can be anywhere on the globe via plane in about a day. Technology enables people to communicate across the world with the click of a button. This has greatly impacted the movement of people groups. For example, M. Daniel Carroll R., in his book dealing with immigration in the West from a Christian perspective, observes, "The greater part of Christians now live outside North America and Western Europe. Some characterize this movement of Christianity's center of gravity as the...'globalizing' of the faith" (*Christians at the Border*, p. 60). Similarly, Andrew Walls also notes, "By 1980, the balance [of Christianity] had shifted again, southwards; Africa is now the continent most notable for those that profess and call themselves Christians" (*The Missionary Movement in Christian History*, p. 6). This shift brings with it contemporary issues which the western church will have to work through. Not least of these issues involves the role of hospitality and the American church's place in welcoming others from around the globe.

Awareness of this southward shift is present and still growing in the West. The landscape has changed but continues to evolve. What role will the West take in this as a result? One point is clear: The American church can either embrace the shift or deny it. If the latter is chosen then the American church could potentially miss out on a great spiritual opportunity—perhaps even spiritual renewal. If "pride-of-place" is maintained by the American church, thus fighting against or ignoring the global shift within Christianity and all the potential benefits and opportunities for growth, then stagnation or even further decline among some segments of American Christianity seems possible. As Ogletree warns, "Ethnocentricity is egoism in cultural mode" (*Hospitality to the Stranger*, p. 49). Further, Carroll reminds us that a surprising number of immigrants, migrants and refugees are Christians (*Christians at the Border*, pp. 60-61). This information is potentially vital for the American church which currently finds itself in the midst of figuring out where to land in issues related to immigration.

Indeed, many scholars, including Soong-Chan Rah, hold strongly to the conviction that "immigrants and ethnic minorities are saving American Christianity" (*The Next Evangelicalism*, p. 74). To fail to pay any attention to this reality in America could possibly mean to miss out on the work of God in this nation. Taking the issue further, Parker Palmer writes, "Deeper still, the public life is an arena of spiritual experience, a setting in which God speaks to us and forms our hearts with words we cannot hear in the private realm. If we deprive ourselves of public experience, we deny ourselves a unique and compelling form of spiritual growth, a unique and compelling sort of communion with God" (*The Company of Strangers*, p. 63). In light of this, hospitality is a potential key for growth and health of the American church.

The American church finds itself at a peculiar but important crossroad regarding its path and potentially even its identity. Christine Pohl writes, "For a number of centuries, both hospitality and alien status remained crucial to the identity of the church. Early apologists for the Christian faith pointed to the way Christians lived in the world—with extraordinary hospitality while belonging to no society fully—as proof of the truth of Christianity" ("Biblical Issues in Mission and Migration," *Missiology: An International Review*, 31.1, p.8). If Pohl's words are accurate, portions of the American church appear dangerously close to losing their true identity as part of the "people of God." For too much of American Christianity, nativism appears to be the primary response rather than grace and openness (Carroll, *Christians at the Border*, p. 30). Thus the West is potentially missing many God-given opportunities stemming from the large numbers of diaspora people groups living throughout the world, at this time. In our brief assessment of the American church, we must be careful not to overreact and make things out to be worse than they actually are. While it is true that mainline denominations are declining, this is not necessarily true for the rest of the Church in America. On his blog, *The Exchange*, Ed Stetzer states, for example, "The church is not dying…While I believe we need to understand reality inside our ranks, I don't believe the situation is quite as dire as many are making it out to be. Actually, no serious researcher believes Christianity in America is dying. Not one" (Stetzer, "The State of the Church in America" *The Exchange* [Blog]). Stetzer accounts for this by pointing to several factors. First, he points to American Religious Identification Survey (ARIS) of 2009. According to this survey, writes Stetzer, "self identified Christians had fallen 10 percentage points, from 86 to 76, since 1990." A second factor, argues Stetzer, is that the ARIS "showed that the 'Nones'—those who claim no religious affiliation—rose from 8 to 15 percent." This leads Stetzer to posit that the apparent death of the American church can, in some sense, be identified as the church "just being more clearly defined." This possibly accounts for some of what is happening within the American church today. However, there is certainly more at play as well. For instance, it could perhaps be argued that most mainline churches have found themselves divorced in a sense from Jesus Christ. In the name of tolerance and inclusivity there is the risk of accepting everything and thus stripping anything of meaning. Another potential result in such churches is a lack of deep and lasting relationship. A church without deep relationship will struggle to be a truly hospitable community of Christ.

THE CHALLENGE OF WEALTH AND PRIVILEGE

Another contemporary issue pertains to affluence and mistrust. Jonathan J. Bonk, in his work *Missions and Money*, demonstrates that throughout the history of western church missions, the motives of missionaries have not always been gospel-centered. Many went to distant shores for financial gain or to make a name for themselves. This has led to a host of issues relevant to our study. As Bonk sums up, "With affluence comes social advantage; with social advantage comes personal security and power—power over those with less, power over one's own destiny, the power of choice" (*Missions and Money*, p. 64). American pastor David Platt illustrates Bonk's thought in his book Radical, when he shares about a church newsletter celebrating two items on its front page: (1) $5,000 raised to help refugees in Sudan and (2) a new $23 million church building (p. 16). This is an indicator that the western church is misaligned with God's original intent, desire, and mission for it. As Elizabeth Newman points out, "The key point here is that our scientific/economic culture forms us to live lives of detachment" (*Untamed Hospitality*, p. 76). In other words, it would appear that the American church has done a decent job at compartmentalizing its faith. This, as a result, has left little, if any, room for hospitality to develop as a forerunning characteristic of the American church.

A NEW CALL TO HOSPITALITY

Are things really this grim for the American church? I hold that American Christianity still has much to offer the Majority World, but Christians in America must embrace the present challenges and hospitality is, it would seem, a key to the overall success and evolution of the American church at this time. To quote Elizabeth Newman, "[Hospitality] is rather a practice, at once ecclesial and public, embodying a politics, economics, and ethics at odds with dominant cultural assumptions" (*Untamed Hospitality*, p. 14).

Hospitality, by its very nature, forces one to face issues of globalization, privilege and wealth. Perhaps it is time for American Christians to re-think the finer points of biblical hospitality.

HOSPITALITY AND CHURCH MULTIPLICATION MOVEMENTS (CMM)

An example of a believer who has embraced or harnessed the potential of hospitality is South Africa's Bruce Bennett. Bennett leads a team of missionaries and church planters called One Mission Society who have developed a system of church planting that has witnessed dramatic growth throughout Africa and Asia. As I write, Bennett's latest report shares that now 3.9 million members and 35,000 churches have been planted since his system was implemented nearly ten years ago. Bennett's system is defined as a church multiplication movement (CMM). The system involves planting churches which then reproduce more churches. Many of the churches planted through Bennett's system have reproduced three and four times or more. The major components to Bennett's system revolve around the twin concepts of hospitality and the "person of peace," which will be examined more deeply in Chapter 5.

This brings us to several important questions that indicate the need for our study of hospitality as essential for carrying out missions in America. The first question deals with the sustainability of hospitality in America as the culture currently stands. Can a system built on and around hospitality be sustained in a culture that seems to be focused on individualism? Second, what role does the concept of "family" play within this picture? Hospitality, by nature, is short-term; the concept of family is long-term. What shifts and changes in our understanding and thinking will need to be made in order to embrace a lifestyle of hospitality? And third, is this really hospitality? Hospitality by nature has the element of surprise. There is uncertainty as to when or where one will encounter or entertain a stranger. Also, does the notion of hospitality and the "person of peace," as we will see with Bruce Bennett's system, bring a priori notions along with it that nullify the nature of biblical hospitality?

Finally, we will address what may be the "elephant in the room" regarding this topic: Will it work in the West?

Regarding the need for this study, the shift in World Christianity from the West to the global South suggests this time in history represents an important turning point for America and the entire world. Before looking at what the Bible has to say about hospitality, a couple of preliminary comments should be made at this point. First, in light of the current globalization and large scale movements of people groups, the American church must awaken to the important biblical teaching surrounding hospitality. It would appear that the American church is being presented with an opportunity to come alongside the Global Church and journey together through which hospitality will prove important. Furthermore, we should be more hospitable because it is an overflow of the love we have for God and others. Douglas H. Knight warns us against the possible outcomes of rejecting hospitality:

> By not receiving this specific mediation that God provides, we are rendering ourselves less and less able to take anything else that is given. Since our whole action has come to deny the being and significance of this people, we are less able to receive or acknowledge the being and otherness of any people. Without the aid God provides, we become more enfeebled and less able to perceive and receive otherness in any form. Our own being dwindles away" (*The Eschatological Economy*, p. 21).

Second, it seems that year after year, the American church is decreasing in numbers as well as in influence. Could a reawakening to biblical hospitality that honors God and Jesus Christ as Host and the other as ourselves help breathe new life back into what appears to be a decaying body? I believe wholeheartedly that this renewal can happen, if hospitality is once again understood and embraced.

CHAPTER 2:

GOD AS HOST IN THE OLD TESTAMENT

The proper place to begin our inquiry into what the Bible has to say about hospitality is with God himself. Biblical hospitality is rooted in God's nature. As our examination will show, we can understand the essence of hospitality through God's interactions with people because God, as part of his very being, is hospitable. We will not comprehensively examine this topic in the Old Testament, but we will assess some of its pertinent passages in order to lay the groundwork for the latter portion of this study. As noted above, the word hospitality does not appear in any Old Testament text nor in the Septuagint. In light of this, we will examine passages that exhibit demonstrations of hospitality.

GOD'S HOSPITALITY TOWARD ADAM AND EVE —GENESIS 1:26-31; 2:7-9, 15-17

The early chapters of the book of Genesis show that hospitality is rooted in God's nature. The reader encounters God, the One who created all things ex nihilo. As the account reads, God formed the heavens and the earth over a six day period. Water, dry land, lights, vegetation and every living creature find its ontological existence stemming from the will of the Creator. The account reaches its pinnacle on the sixth day. Genesis 1:26-31, arguably the final act of creation, describes how humanity is made in the image of its Creator:

> Then God said, "Let us make mankind in our image, in our likeness, so that they may rule over the fish in the sea and the birds in the sky, over the livestock and all the wild animals, and over all the creatures that move along the ground." So God created mankind in his own image, in the image of God he created them; male and female he created them (Gen. 1:26-27).

I would argue that this is possibly the first instance of recorded hospitality in the Bible. According to the rules of hospitality, God fulfills the role of "host" while humanity is invited through the creative work of God into the role of "guest." In the words of Douglas H. Knight, "God is our host," and "He has made himself known to us as our host" (*The Eschatological Economy*, p. 23). Within his creative work, God is revealing himself to his creation as the Divine Host. As Divine Host, God shares with his "guests" something of great value—his image. Within this portrait of hospitality we find humanity receiving a welcome from the Divine Host and subsequently, in this welcome, humanity finds its very identity.

Christine D. Pohl holds that the account of Abraham welcoming three visitors in Genesis 18:1-15 is the "first formative story of the biblical tradition on hospitality" (*Making Room*, p. 24). If our interpretation is correct, the opening chapters of Genesis reveal the biblical precedent for hospitality. Pohl argues that hospitality is connected with God's presence, promise, and blessing (*Making Room*, p. 24). I contend that all three of these themes are present in the early chapters of Genesis. As Creator, God's presence permeates the creation account. According to Genesis 1:28, we witness humanity receiving a blessing while experiencing the presence of God through dialogue: "God blessed them and said to them, 'Be fruitful and increase in number; fill the earth and subdue it. Rule over the fish in the sea and the birds in the sky and over every living creature that moves on the ground.'" This blessing also includes the provision of food (Gen. 1:29-30). As for the promise, perhaps Genesis 2:16-17 addresses this aspect: "And the Lord God commanded the man, 'You are free to eat from any tree in the garden; but you must not eat from the tree of the knowledge of good and evil, for when you eat from it you will certainly die.'"

Furthermore, a portion of God's role as "host" can be seen through the created order itself. God creates all things in six days. If humanity, as sharing in his image, is the pinnacle of his creation why does he wait to create them last? The answer, I believe, lies in God as Divine Host. He was preparing the world, making it just right, in order for humanity to live and flourish under his great abundance. As seen in God's nature, a portrait of the Garden of Eden depicts his great abundance. The fact that after everything God creates, he calls it "good" (Gen. 1:10, 12, 18, 21, 25, 31) supports this. "Our worship of God," Elizabeth Newman states, "rests on the fact that in the beginning there is always gift, the overflow of God's eternal triune communion. In worship . . . we learn to be God's guests and hosts" (*Untamed Hospitality*, p. 45). According to Genesis, humanity is not created merely as an afterthought, as is depicted in other ancient creation accounts, such as the *Enuma Elish*:

> Arteries I will knot
> and bring bones into being.
> I will create Lullu, "man" be his name
> I will form Lullu, man
> Let him be burdened with the toil of the gods,
> that they may freely breath—
> They bound him (Kingu), held him before Ea
> inflicted the penalty on him,
> severed his arteries;
> and from his blood he formed mankind
> imposed toil on man, set the gods free.
> (Jacobsen, *Treasures*, pp. 180-181 cited in Hamilton, *Genesis 1-17*, p. 140.)

In the *Enuma Elish*, humanity was made solely as a servant for the gods and without dignity, being fashioned from the blood of the defeated god, Kingu. As is evident from Genesis 1:28-30, and in contrast with the *Enuma Elish*, God creates humanity with dignity, purpose, mission and dominion over the created order, and in his image! Thus, as Divine Host, God creates all things and lastly creates humanity in order to invite humanity to participate with him in what he has abundantly made. Furthermore, the blessing of Genesis 1:28-30, as John Walton argues, "must be recognized as delineating a privilege, not an obligation. In the ancient world, the ability to reproduce was seen as a gift from God" (Genesis, p. 134). This gift is further evidence of the hospitality of God toward humanity.

God's role as Divine Host is continued in Genesis 2:7-9. These verses supply further commentary on the creation of humanity initially depicted in Genesis 1:26-31. Genesis 2:7 records that God "formed a man from the dust of the ground and breathed into his nostrils the breath of life, and the man became a living being." Being raised from the dust demonstrates the hospitality of God. "To be 'raised from the dust,'" according to John Walton, "means to be elevated to royal office, to rise above poverty, to find life" (*Genesis*, p. 158). Within this life-giving breath from God to humanity we find the heart of hospitality. In it, we encounter what we could possibly refer to as "the great invitation." In giving the breath of life to humanity, God freely invites humanity to enter into his very own space—his creation. "By definition," writes Christine Pohl, "hospitality involves some space into which people are welcomed, a place where unless invitation is given, the stranger would not feel free to enter" (*Making Room*, p. 39). In *The Temple in the Church's Mission,* Greg Beale argues that "Eden was the first archetypal temple" (pp.79-80). If this is true, then it is significant for our study. The indication would be that the Garden of Eden was not merely the created home of humanity—it was God's "home," his dwelling place with humanity. From this perspective, one could view the creation account as God demonstrating his heart as Divine Host by inviting humanity into a space (God's presence) in which there was no previous access.

In light of what we have discussed thus far regarding the biblical creation account as rooting hospitality in God's own nature, we can perhaps glean a fresh perspective on the fall of humanity as recorded in Genesis 3. If what we have stated so far is accurate, then the decision and subsequent behavior of Adam and Eve is the ultimate rejection of it. In the fall, we see the rejection of God's hospitality. Humanity rejected God by attempting to "be like him" on their own accord (Gen. 3:5). In this act humanity rejected God's abundant blessings resulting in expulsion from his presence (Gen. 3:23). This expulsion also resulted in scarcity of food, water and even God's presence (Gen. 3:17-19). Now humanity would have to tend soil that also produces thistles and thorns, with God's abundant presence and fruit found within the garden no longer available to them. What is more, Genesis 3:24 indicates that access to the garden was closed off: "After he drove the man out, he placed on the east side of the Garden of Eden cherubim and a flaming sword flashing back and forth to guard the way to the tree of life." Closing off the way back into the garden is also significant in terms of hospitality. Christine Pohl writes that "a door—opened or closed—is one of the most powerful images of hospitality" (*Making Room*, p. 131). Hospitality exercised properly places responsibility upon both the guest and the host. Humanity, according to Genesis 2:15, was given responsibility to "stand guard" over the garden (Greg Beale, *The Temple in the Church's Mission*, p. 66). Additionally, by warning humanity not to eat from the Tree of Knowledge (Gen. 2:16-17), God behaves as the ideal host by placing healthy boundaries upon his guests. As Pohl observes, this balance between the role of guest and host is vital for hospitality to function properly (*Making Room*, p. 145). It was precisely this balance that was broken according to Genesis 3. In *The Book of Genesis*, Chapters 1-17, Victor Hamilton pinpoints this as the source of the damaged relationship between guest and host: "One's choices should not be made in the interests of the self. Rather, such choices should be made within the range of God's directives" (p. 211). Interpreted through the lens of hospitality, the creation of all things can be viewed as God's great invitation, inviting humanity to participate with him within his "space." Meanwhile, the fall of humanity can be viewed as its ultimate rejection of God's hospitality resulting in dismissal from God's "space."

THE WILDERNESS WANDERINGS—EXODUS 15:22-27

God's hospitality toward people can again be seen in the wilderness wanderings of the Israelites after their Exodus from Egypt. Following the miraculous parting of the Red Sea, the crossing on dry land, the destruction of Pharaoh and his army, and the subsequent celebration (Exod. 13:17-15:21), we find the Israelites wandering through the Desert of Shur. For three days they wander with no supply of water (Exod. 15:22). The Israelites finally arrive at Marah only to find the available water supply too bitter to drink (Exod. 15:23). After the people grumble to Moses, he looks to Yahweh who in turn shows him what to do in order to make the bitter water clean (Exod. 15:23-25a). Here God's hospitality comes to the fore.

The Israelites present with a need, water, and God sustains them with clean water. Additionally, he provides manna and quail for the Israelites to eat (Exod. 16:1-36) as well as more water, this time from a rock, to meet their need (Exod. 17:1-7). We will focus our attention on Exodus 15:22-27.

Interestingly, in The Literary Structure of the Old Testament, David Dorsey draws a parallel between this passage and Genesis 1-11 by identifying a seven-part chiastic structure stretching from Genesis 1 to Exodus 19:2. In Dorsey's structure, Genesis 1-11 and Exodus 13:17-19:2 represent the opening and closing points. In the first point, we witness "primeval history: Yahweh's power in creation and the flood"; in the closing point, we witness "wilderness journey: Yahweh's power in the desert" (*The Literary Structure of the Old Testament*, p. 70). What makes this pertinent to our study is how Yahweh behaves hospitably toward his people in both instances. For example, in the both situations, God meets the needs of his people by providing a source of food. Even though humanity has rejected his hospitality, as represented by Adam and Eve's behavior in the Garden, God continually shows hospitality to his people, because hospitality appears to be part of his nature. Dorsey concludes, "[Yahweh] is the one who has repeatedly protected and rescued [his people] and the same power he demonstrated in Egypt against mighty pharaoh will continue to be available to his people when they find themselves in other vulnerable circumstances" (*The Literary Structure of the Old Testament*, p. 71). The character of Yahweh, from Genesis to the Wilderness Wanderings, is marked by hospitality. God is the consummate Host continually providing for his people.

Exodus 15:22-27 is pertinent to the topic of hospitality for another reason. Exodus 15:25b tells us that, "There the Lord issued a ruling and instruction for them and put them to the test."

The practice of hospitality occasionally involved a test for those potentially receiving it to ensure they were worthy recipients. (cf. Walter A. Vogels, "Hospitality in Biblical Perspective," *Liturgical Ministry*, 11 [2002], p. 171). The test is explicitly stated in Exodus 15:26 and can be summed up with the word obedience: "If you listen carefully to the Lord your God and do what is right in his eyes, if you pay attention to his commands and keep all his decrees, I will not bring on you any of the diseases I brought on the Egyptians, for I am the Lord, who heals you." God was testing his people specifically to see if they were obedient and thus worthy recipients of his hospitality. Peter Enns likewise sees a deeper perspective to this testing: "God wants to produce in his people a deepening relationship with him as their covenant God so that they will better understand the importance of keeping the Sabbath, the other commands, and the need to trust him daily. This is what it means for God to test his people" (*Exodus*, p. 332). It appears that both God's hospitality and testing of his people are for the greater purpose of producing a deeper lasting relationship. However, just as Adam and Even rejected God's hospitality, the Israelites also turn their situation against God. "The problem is not so much that the Israelites 'fail' the test, but that they turn around and put God to the test " (Enns, *Exodus*, p. 332, emphasis his). In the paradigm of hospitality this action by the Israelites runs counter to the nature of hospitality. In light of this, the Israelites' putting God to the test is similar to the action of Adam and Eve in Genesis. Both actually test or reject the hospitality of God.

Before leaving this passage, we must make one final observation. Exodus 15 closes with this: "Then they came to Elim, where there were twelve springs and seventy palm trees, and they camped near the water." In this chapter, then, we are presented with the need (Exod. 15:22-24), God's provision of hospitality (Exod. 15:25a), the test (Exod. 15:25b-26) and finally a foretaste of the promise resulting from the test (Exod. 15:27). As a culmination of the Israelites' obedience to the test, God promises to bring them healing. The wilderness was viewed as a dangerous place. God graciously gives his people a foretaste at Elim of what is to come when they properly respond to his hospitality. As noted above, God's greater purpose was the development of a lasting relationship with his people. The role of hospitality and the related testing of his people are essential tools of God, rooted in his very character, and serve as the means of developing this lasting relationship. In light of this, the provision found at Elim, while being very real and immediate, also offer a "glimpse of what is to come, the lush land of Canaan, the land God promised to the patriarchs and which he has prepared for his people" (Enns, *Exodus*, p. 324). The experiences of the Israelites in the wilderness foreshadow the blessings of hospitality God has in store for Israel in the Promise Land. When they eventually settle in this land there will be a switch from guest to host. As Amos Yong states:

> Israel remains ever a group of sojourners in the eyes of God, as it is God who also owns the land and all that is in it that is given to Israel (Lev. 25:23). And as perpetual sojourners, Israel not only had the responsibility to care for the strangers in her midst, but also the opportunity to receive, even the blessings of Yahweh, from them (Amos Yong, *Hospitality and the Other*, p. 110).

While God's people will always be fully reliant upon him as Host, God is also preparing them for future interactions with others who will be their guests, such as the foreigners and aliens living in their midst.

GOD AS SHEPHERD—PSALM 23

Numerous psalms also point out the hospitality of Yahweh and the dependence of humanity upon Him. Because of the space limitations of our study, we will narrow our focus to Psalm 23 in particular. Before we look at the psalm, it is of benefit to note that Psalm 23 is replete with imagery that reappears throughout Psalms 24-30 (Gerald H. Wilson, *Psalms*, 1:431). This connection may suggest that this entire block of psalms exemplifies the hospitality of Yahweh in his relationship with his people.

For our examination of Psalm 23, we will divide the psalm into two sections: verses 1-4 and verses 5-6. In the first section, Yahweh is depicted as Shepherd. He guides his sheep to food and water (v. 2), on right paths (v. 3), and through dark valleys, protects them and comforts them (v. 4). He takes great care to ensure that his sheep have all of their needs met (v. 1). As Shepherd, Yahweh appears here as the great Host or "provider" (Gerald H. Wilson, *Psalms*, 1:433).

While hospitality is not specifically mentioned, its themes permeate this section of Psalm 23. A test for the sheep is implied. It is found in the need to trust. Yahweh's people must trust in him as sheep would fully trust their shepherd (Gerald H. Wilson, *Psalms*, 1:432). The results for those sheep are clear: food, water, comfort, rest, the right path and the basic needs of life are in the beneficent hands of the Shepherd.

The themes of hospitality continue throughout the second section of Psalm 23. There is, however, a change in the overall imagery. This section, consisting of verses 5-6, shift from Shepherd/sheep imagery to Host/guest imagery. Yahweh is now depicted as the Host while his people fulfill the role of guest. Yahweh as Host continues to express his hospitable character: (1) preparing a table for his guest in the presence of the guest's enemies, (2) anointing the guest with oil, (3) filling the guest's cup to overflowing, which culminates in (4) "the realization of ultimate communion with God himself" (Gerald H. Wilson, *Psalms*, 1:436). Again, as with the first section of this Psalm, although no sort of test is mentioned, it does seem to imply one. Once again the test involves trust. The guest must demonstrate trust in the host. In this instance, the test of trust is demonstrated in the form of the Host preparing a table for the guest in the presence of the guest's enemies (Gerald H. Wilson, *Psalms*, 1:436). This test may also recall the exodus from Egypt, precisely the moment when the Israelites stood next to the Red Sea while Pharaoh's army approached. That, too, was a time of trust on behalf of Israel for Yahweh to provide.

There is another, perhaps deeper, picture of hospitality at work in these verses. "To accept another as a guest at one's table," writes

Wilson, "was to set aside enmity and to assume responsibility for the safety of the guest while in your dwelling" (Wilson, *Psalms*, p. 436). This portrait of hospitality points to the ongoing relationship that Yahweh desires with his people. We have seen this motif at work in the Garden with Adam and Eve and in Yahweh's interaction with Israel during their wilderness wanderings. Just as in those instances, Yahweh works to develop deeper relationship with his people through the means of hospitality. Ultimately, as Wilson puts it, "to dwell with God is a potent image of eternal security and ongoing relationship" (Gerald H. Wilson, *Psalms*, 1:437). This ongoing security and relationship seems to comprise a core component of hospitality. This aspect of hospitality is revealed to us through God's interactions with Israel, namely in the way he provides for his people.

CHAPTER 3:

HUMANS AS HOSTS IN THE OLD TESTAMENT

We will now concentrate our attention on humanity fulfilling the role of host in the Old Testament. Since hospitality is rooted in the nature of God, it seems axiomatic that we should see the same principles of hospitality at work among people, the pinnacle of God's creation.

THE EXAMPLE OF ABRAHAM—GENESIS 18:1-15

As mentioned earlier, Christine Pohl holds that this passage is the first biblical example of hospitality. While we have not necessarily subscribed to that thought, it is nevertheless an important Old Testament passage for understanding the concept of hospitality. There is one significant reversal here, however, as humanity, in this instance, Abraham, plays the role of host, while Yahweh is the guest.

The passage begins with Abraham sitting at the entrance to his tent under the shade of trees during the hottest portion of the day (18:1-2). In verse 1, we are told that "The Lord appeared to Abraham." In verse 2, Abraham looks up and sees three men nearby. John Walton notes this is a theophany, but Abraham does not appear to recognize it (Walton, *Genesis*, p. 452). Abraham does, however, recognize his role as host to these guests. Walter Vogels observes that within the ancient practice of hospitality, the guest was viewed as sacred by the host ("Hospitality in Biblical Perspective," *Liturgical Ministry*, vol. 11, fall 2002, p. 168). Abraham's response to the three men standing nearby illustrates this: "When he saw them, he hurried from the entrance of his tent to meet them and bowed low to the ground" (18:2). Abraham's "hurrying" and "bowing" demonstrate a servant's posture toward the strangers. As Vogels asserts:

As a good host Abraham must pay respect to his guests, and that is what he does: "As soon as he saw them he ran from the entrance of the tent to meet them, and bowed down to the ground" (v. 2). The verbs stress Abraham's hospitality. Instead of going inside and closing his home to the visitors, he runs toward them like a person does to welcome a member of the family whom he has not seen for a long time (Gen 29:13; 33:4; Luke 15:20). Abraham bows to the ground in a gesture of respect (Gen 23:12; 42:6). Everything follows the rules of hospitality at that time. The first words Abraham addresses to the visitors are: "My Lord, if I have found favor in your eyes, please do not pass your servant by" (v. 3). This seems like a reversal of roles; the guest is called "my Lord," while the host calls himself "your servant"; indeed, the host puts himself at the service of his guests (p. 165).

Numerous aspects of hospitality play out in this passage. In verses 2-3, we find the "warm welcome/invitation." Verse 4 mentions the common hospitable act of "foot washing." Abraham offers the strangers water to cleanse their feet from the journey. This verse also mentions the component of "protection," as Abraham offers them the opportunity to rest under the shade of the trees. Verse 5 has the "feeding or feasting" component of hospitality. Here Abraham offers the guests something to eat so that they may be refreshed as they continue on with their journey. This last component, in particular, parallels the abundant hospitality of Yahweh we have seen earlier. While Abraham offers to feed the strangers, he does not mention what food he will give them or how much. What Abraham does provide for the guests to eat, however, is rather extravagant. The three seahs of fine flour for the baking of bread (v. 6), along with the choice and tender calf for meat (v. 7), as well as curds and milk seems to be more than "the three visitors, Sara, and Abraham can possibly eat" (Victor P. Hamilton, *The Book of Genesis*, Chapters 18-50, p. 11). As Yahweh demonstrated abundant hospitality within the creation account toward humanity and throughout the history of the Israelites, similarly Abraham exhibits abundant hospitality toward the three strangers within this theophanic encounter.

Following the opening display of hospitality in this passage (Gen. 18:1-8), in which Abraham plays the host, there is an interesting reversal of sorts. Initially, the stranger is addressed as "Lord" and the host is addressed as "servant." However, in the remainder of the passage (Gen. 18:9-15), the guest actually blesses the host. In this case the guest blesses the host by way of a promise: "Then one of them said, 'I will surely return to you about this time next year, and Sarah your wife will have a son'" (Gen. 18:10, 14). Yahweh has promised Abraham and Sarah a son previously (cf. Gen. 15:4; 17:16), but now the promise is definitive ("about this time next year").

In the practice of hospitality, the host is not to pressure or expect anything from the guest. Nevertheless, as Vogels notes, it was not uncommon for a guest to share news, express thanksgiving, give a blessing, or to wish the host good luck in response ("Hospitality in Biblical Perspective," *Liturgical Ministry*, Vol. 11. Fall 2002, p.166). This is precisely what transpires between the hospitable interaction between Abraham and the three strangers. The literary structure of Genesis emphasizes this thought. According to Dorsey, Genesis 12:1-21:7 comprises a literary unit which he entitles "Abraham and the promise of a son" (*Literary Structure*, p. 56). As one can see, the role of hospitality enacted by Abraham with the three strangers plays a role in God's final reiteration of the promise to give Abraham and Sarah a son.

THE EXAMPLE OF LOT—GENESIS 19:1-13

At first blush, this passage can appear to raise more questions than it answers. However, the lens of hospitality may help to make more sense of the passage. It begins with Lot sitting at the gate to the city of Sodom. While Lot is sitting there "two angels" arrive on the scene. Lot's response, Walter Vogels observes, rings similar to the response of Abraham toward the visitors in Genesis 18:2 ("Hospitality in Biblical Perspective," *Liturgical Ministry*, Vol. 11. Fall 2002, p. 167). As Abraham had gotten up, run to the visitors, and bowed down before them, in similar fashion, Lot, upon seeing the two visitors, "got up to meet them and bowed down with his face to the ground" (19:1). Furthermore, as Abraham addressed his guests as "Lord" and himself as their "servant," Lot does likewise. Lot addresses the two angels as "My lords" and himself as "your servant" (Gen. 19:2). Other components of hospitality present themselves in this passage as well. Lot offers the two guests an opportunity to have their feet washed, rest/protection, and food by opening his home to them for the night (v. 2).

Interestingly, while in the Abraham account the guests accept the invitation to hospitality, here Lot's guests initially refuse (19:2), which was well within their rights and in accordance with the rules of hospitality (Vogels, "Hospitality in Biblical Perspective," *Liturgical Ministry*, Vol. 11. Fall 2002, p.167). But Lot persists ("he insisted so strongly"), and the two guests eventually agree to accept his generosity for the evening (v. 3). While in the home, Lot continues in the role of host by preparing a meal for his guests. However, his role as hospitable host was about to be tested before the evening came to an end.

In 18:4-5, the tone of the story quickly changes: "Before they had gone to bed, all the men from every part of the city of Sodom—both young and old—surrounded the house. They called to Lot, 'Where are the men who came to you tonight? Bring them out here so we can have sex with them.'" The bulk of interpretive issues surrounding this passage revolve around the Hebrew root yd'. Victor Hamilton suggests that this word is used 948 times in the Old Testament as a verb referring to sexual knowledge (*The Book of Genesis*, Chapters 18-50, p. 33). The debate falls basically between two camps: (1) the men declare that Lot turn his guests over to the mob for sexual exploitation (i.e., as the NIV translates - "so we can have sex with them") or (2) the Sodomites are actually breaching the rules of hospitality.

John H. Walton weighs in on this passage when he states:

> The sin of the Sodomites is self-evident, blatant and un-
> ambiguous . . . There is nothing subtle or secretive about their

behavior. No inhibitions interfere with their threats of violence or demands to indulge in their lust. The last thing anyone in the reading audience would be expected to do would be to come to the defense of Sodom or try to make excuses for their behavior (*Genesis*, pp. 476–477).

In spite of the tone of this passage one can still see the implications of hospitality at work. The gathered men of Sodom break the rules of hospitality by threatening to break down Lot's door, calling him a "foreigner" (19:9). To rape a guest is certainly inhospitable. Even if the men of Sodom where merely desiring to interrogate and imprison the guests, that action would still be inhospitable (cf. Scott Morschauser, "Hospitality,' Hostiles and Hostages: On the Legal Background of Genesis 19:1-9." *Journal for the Study of the Old Testament*, vol. 27 no 4. June 2003, pp. 461-85). Lot, on the other hand, does not give over his daughters (even though he offered) nor does he give up his guests. Lot is actually a good host.

Just as there was a promise of blessing that resulted in Abraham's hospitality, there is likewise a blessing that is given to Lot and his family. According to Genesis 19:10, the two strangers pull Lot back into the house and close the door, thus saving Lot from the threat of the crowd. The two guests then warn Lot to get his family out of Sodom because Yahweh has sent them to destroy the city (Gen. 19:12). Whereas Abraham's hospitality resulted in the promise of a child, Lot's hospitality resulted in the salvation of his and his daughters' lives.

THE ENCOUNTER BETWEEN ABRAHAM'S SERVANT AND REBEKAH—GENESIS 24

One final example of hospitality in the Old Testament that we will look at is the account of Abraham's servant's encounter with Rebekah at the well.

After Sarah's death (Gen. 23) and Abraham's descent into "very old" (Gen. 24:1), Abraham focuses attention on finding a wife for his son, Isaac. Abraham sends out one of his servants to find a suitable wife for Isaac (Gen. 24:1-9). The servant arrives at a well outside of the town of Nahor (Gen. 24:10), where he stops to allow his camels to rest. Evening was approaching, which was the time the women would venture out to the well to draw water (Gen. 24:11). At this time, Abraham's servant prays to Yahweh, thus laying out a test, not only for Yahweh but also for the approaching women that would involve hospitality (Gen. 24:12-14). The test involved two specific aspects: the woman (1) obliging the servant's request for a drink and (2) offering the camels a drink.

Rebekah arrives at the well, and Abraham's servant "hurries to meet her" and asks for a drink of water (Gen. 24:17). Even though the servant is the one receiving the hospitality, this language appears reminiscent of both Abraham and Lot hurrying to meet the strangers in the accounts examined above (cf. Gen. 18:2; 19:1). Rebekah responds without hesitation to the servant's request by providing him with a drink and then immediately turning to offer water to his camels, thus passing the test involving hospitality (Gen. 24:19-21). Victor Hamilton draws out the parallel of the hospitable nature in this encounter between Abraham and Rebekah when he writes, "In her behavior [Rebekah] is reflecting the quick and hospitable actions of her father-in-law-to-be" (*The Book of Genesis*, Chapters 18-50, p. 147).

Rebekah's passing of this test leads to even more hospitality. Following the incident at the well, Rebekah now gives an invitation to Abraham's servant to stay at her family's home. Rebekah states, "We have plenty of straw and fodder, as well as room for you to spend the night" (Gen. 24:25). Hamilton sees a correlation between this encounter and the one with Lot: "Rebekah's effusive nature is attested by the fact that she offers not only to water the servant's camels but to feed them as well. In this respect she is like Lot, who opened his home willingly to strangers" (*The Book of Genesis*, Chapters 18-50, p. 148). After the invitation is given, Rebekah hurries home (cf. Gen. 24:18) to inform her family that a stranger is coming to visit (Gen. 24:28-31). Upon arriving at Rebekah's home, the hosts proceed to provide food for the camels and water for Abraham's servant and the men traveling with him to wash their feet (Gen. 24:32-33).

The result of this encounter appears similar to the results of the hospitality displayed by Abraham and Lot. Abraham and Sarah were given the promise of a child even though they were well along in years (Gen. 18:10-11). Lot and his daughters were spared from the destruction which was brought on Sodom and Gomorrah (19:12-13, 29). Here, although with a reversal of sort since the servant is actually the guest, the result is a divinely arranged marriage (Gen. 24:67). Rebekah, in the end, is given permission to return with the servant to become Isaac's wife (Gen. 24:50-51).

Throughout this episode, the reader can see that it is actually Yahweh working through human hospitality to bring about his will. We can see this in two ways. As noted by Hamilton, the servant worships Yahweh on three different occasions: Gen. 24:12-14, 26, 52 (*The Book of Genesis, Chapters 18-50*, p. 158). Perhaps the language utilized by Laban, Rebekah's brother, points to Yahweh as the guide behind the servant's commission to find a wife for Isaac (p. 156). For example, when Laban meets Abraham's servant he addresses him by saying, "Come, you who are blessed by the Lord" (Gen. 24:31a). Furthermore, when Laban agrees to allow Rebekah to return with the servant he says, "This is from the Lord, we can say nothing to you one way or the other. Here is Rebekah; take her and go, and let her become the wife of your master's son, as the Lord has directed" (Gen. 24:50-51). Although, on the other hand it could be argues that Laban is a questionable host due to his attempts to extort the servant on several occasions. Nevertheless, hospitality plays a role in this scene and its subsequent results.

There is one other aspect to this encounter we should draw attention to. At the outset, Abraham informs his servant of his missions' directives. As part of his instructions, Abraham says, "The Lord, the God of heaven, who brought me out of my father's household and my native land and who spoke to me and promised me on oath, saying, 'To your offspring I will give this land'—he will send his angel before you so that you can get a wife for my son from there" (Gen. 24:7). In light of the fact that God has previously made a covenant with Abraham, that from him will come a great nation (Gen. 12:2) and that all the people of the earth will be blessed through him (Gen. 12:3), Abraham can now, as Hamilton says, be "confident here because God has already sworn to him" that these promises would be fulfilled (*The Book of Genesis*, Chapters 18-50, p. 141). Thus, Yahweh stands behind this entire scene in order to bring about what he had promised to Abraham. From the marriage of Isaac and Rebekah God would work to fulfill the oath he promised—to make Abraham into a great nation and a blessing to all the nations of the earth.

Specific components within our paradigm of hospitality are at work in the Rebekah narrative as well to fulfill a greater purpose—a marriage that will result in twelve sons who will become the twelve tribes of Israel: (1) a test involving hospitality, (2) an invitation to come and stay for a brief period of time, (3) the offer of shelter to the stranger for the night, (4) food, for both the stranger and his animals, and (5) water for the stranger and his travelling companions to wash their feet.

CONCLUSION

We have seen in our analysis of several Old Testament accounts that Yahweh has revealed himself as Divine Host. This is especially pronounced within the creation account in Genesis 1-3. God reveals himself as a gracious Divine Host by creating humans after he prepared creation for their arrival. By giving life to humans, inviting them into the Garden of Eden, and inviting them into His very presence, God portrays himself as generous Host toward his creation. Furthermore, God's creation itself is perfect and full of abundant life and food for humanity to use and steward. In light of this, the Fall, as recorded in Genesis 3, is the ultimate rejection of Yahweh's hospitality. Humans are expelled from the Garden of Eden, the place were they enjoyed God's presence in deep relationship.

God's hospitable nature is also apparent in the Wilderness Wanderings and in the Psalms. Throughout the Old Testament, God continually provides food, water, guidance and shelter for his people. There is always more than enough food and water, which shows God's abundant hospitality and reflects his nature as Divine

Host. God's ultimate purpose for making himself known to his creation as Divine Host is to build a lasting and deep relationship with humanity.

Likewise, within the Old Testament, people also play the part of host toward others. Abraham invites three strangers to share a meal only to discover that he entertained angels. Lot invited two strangers to find rest and food in his home for a night. He too was unaware that these strangers were angels of God. For Abraham's servant, Rebekah's acts of hospitality validate her as a suitable wife for Isaac. In each of these accounts, Yahweh is involved. In the first encounter, Abraham and Sarah were given the promise of a son. Second, Lot and his family were spared from the destruction of Sodom and Gomorrah. Finally, Rebekah becomes Isaac's wife—an example of Yahweh's continuing commitment to his promise that through Abraham's offspring, the world would be blessed. Whether through direct encounter or mediated through human agency, Yahweh is the hospitable Divine Host who is always providing, guiding, protecting and feeding his people.

CHAPTER 4:

HOSPITALITY WITHIN THE NEW TESTAMENT

DEFINING HOSPITALITY—*PHILOXENOS/PHILOXENIA*

As previously mentioned, the writings of the Old Testament and even the Septuagint do not make any overt reference to hospitality. Within the New Testament, however, the word "hospitality" is translated from the *philoxenos/philoxenia* word group. This word group is often translated as hospitable and hospitality within the pages of the New Testament (Frederick William Danker, *A Greek-English Lexicon of the New Testament and Other Early Christian Literature*, pp.1058).

The act of hospitality within the NT, as we will see, played a vital role in the life of the first-century church. As Amos Yong states:

> Hence while seeing themselves as missionaries the early Christians nevertheless recognized their status as aliens and strangers, guests who needed to conduct themselves in an honorable and blameless manner amidst their hosts (e.g., 1 Peter 2:12). Perhaps it was precisely because of this precarious situation that they took hospitality seriously (e.g., 1 Peter 4:9; cf. 1 Tim. 5:10) (*Hospitality and the Other*, p. 115).

In light of the rapid spread of Christianity, Christ-followers would have been involved with both giving and receiving hospitality as the gospel spread throughout the Mediterranean "house by house." Bruce Malina points out that hospitality was both "urged" and "practiced" toward traveling Christians ("The Received View and What It Cannot Do: III John and Hospitality," *Semeia*, 35, 1986, p. 185). We will begin our analysis of New Testament hospitality by examining the verses which specifically reference hospitality.

Acts 28:7

Acts 28:7 is part of a larger pericope consisting of Acts 28:1-10. The Apostle Paul journeys to Rome under guard in order to stand trial before Caesar. While journeying, the ship wrecks (Acts 27), leaving everyone alive but stranded on the shore of Malta. Once on the island, the locals proceed to show the shipwrecked victims "unusual kindness" (*philanthropian*). The locals build a fire so the survivors can get warm (Acts 28:1-2). While the word "hospitality" is not used, the locals demonstrate it. By building the fire, the locals invite Paul and his group into their space—the island of Malta.

While the locals are starting the fire, Paul assists by gathering wood. As he places wood on the fire, the heat of the fire drives a viper out from the wood which attaches to Paul's hand (Acts 28:3). The locals respond by thinking Paul must be a murderer. F. F. Bruce succinctly captures the thought process of the locals when he writes, "It was plainly the will of heaven that this man must lose his life—no doubt he was a murderer, and Nemesis was on his trail. He had escaped drowning at sea, indeed, but divine Justice was not so easily baffled: she had designed this alternative way of punishing him" (*The Book of Acts*, p. 498). Perhaps this became a test of sorts concerning hospitality: when the viper came out of the fire and bit Paul on the hand, the locals believed that Paul was not worthy of receiving hospitality.

According to Acts 28:5, Paul merely shakes off the viper into the fire and "suffered no ill effects." The locals expected to see Paul die. However, after considerable time passes and nothing happens, they eventually change their view of Paul. Rather than seeing him as a murderer who is incapable of escaping justice, they now view him as a god (F. F. Bruce, *The Book of Acts*, p. 498). Where the locals initially thought Paul failed the test concerning hospitality, in actuality Paul passed with flying colors. "This is a very interesting story," writes Walter Vogels, "as a passerby traveler [Paul] has to undergo a test to verify that he is not a murderer. After Paul passes the test perfectly, the people wonder if he is not a god . . ., and so they have no problems receiving him. What an honor!" ("Hospitality in Biblical Perspective," *Liturgical Ministry*, Vol. 11. Fall 2002, p. 171). This is important in light of what transpires next in the pericope.

In Acts 28:7-10 the entire scene shifts, though the theme of hospitality still remains. In Acts 28:7 the reader is introduced to Publius, "the chief official of the island." Publius welcomes, or invites, Paul and his companions to his home where he shows them "generous hospitality" (*philophronos*; cf. Danker, p. 1060) for three days (Acts 28:7). Between verses 7 and 8 there is a major shift. In the first instance the reader is introduced to Publius' father who is "sick in bed, suffering from fever and dysentery." In verse 8 Paul's role shifts from guest to host. Luke writes: "Paul went in to see him and, after prayer, placed his hands on him and healed him. When this had happened, the rest of the sick on the island came and were cured" (Acts 28:8b-9).

Luke shares the result of this reciprocal hospitality on Malta in Acts 28:10: "They honored us in many ways; and when we were ready to sail, they furnished us with the supplies we needed." Due to Paul's role reversal, the group was "honored in many ways." This reciprocal demonstration of hospitality culminated in one major result: the needed supplies to continue the journey to Rome! This is no small thing. Jesus Christ's disciples will be God's witnesses to the "ends of the earth" under the guiding power of the Holy Spirit. At the time Luke wrote Acts, Rome was viewed as the seat of world power due to the expansive nature of the Roman Empire. Acts ends with Paul under house arrest in Rome preaching the gospel to Gentiles for two years. Acts 28:30-31 seemingly fulfills Acts 1:8. As I. Howard Marshall states, "Nothing that men can do can stop the progress and ultimate victory of the Gospel" (*Acts*, p. 427). We could add to Marshall's point by noting the key place that hospitality plays in furthering Paul's progress, and thus God's mission to see the gospel arrive in Rome. Yong agrees seeing Paul's shift from receiver to giver of hospitality on the island of Malta as an essential component to this passage (*Hospitality and the Other*, p. 137). Thus, in Acts 28:1-10 the mission of God is linked specifically to the role of hospitality.

Romans 12:13

In Romans 12:13, Paul writes, "Share with the Lord's people who are in need. Practice hospitality." Its larger context is Romans 12:9-21. Most scholars divide the passage into two sections: Romans 12:9-13 and 12:14-21. James R. Edwards, for example, refers to the principle of 12:9-13 as "love within the Christian community" and 12:14-21 as "love for the world at large" (*Romans*, p. 291). If Edwards and others are correct, then the injunction to "practice hospitality" (*ten philoxenian diokontes*) would be the final statement of the first section.

In the beginning of verse 13, Paul calls the church at Rome to "share with the Lord's people who are in need." The word "share" is *koinonountes* which means "fellowship." The call here directs the brotherhood of believers to share generously with one another. Douglas Moo holds that Paul is not merely calling believers to fellowship with one another, but to participate in meeting the material needs of one another (*The Epistle to the Romans*, p. 779). According to Acts 18:2, Luke alludes to Emperor Claudius' expulsion of all the Jews from Rome, which occurred around A.D. 49. The Roman historian Suetonius, who lived late in the first century into the middle part of the second century, records that the expulsion stemmed from "disturbances [in Rome] made at the instigation of Chrestus" (referenced by Edwin Yamauchi, *Jesus under Fire*, p. 215). Perhaps "Chrestus" is a misspelling or misunderstanding of "Christos" which would be a reference to Jesus Christ. Some hold that the Jews' expulsion from Rome was a direct result of Christian missionary activity among the Jews in Rome at the time. The lifting of the ban a few years later could have caused a divide between Jewish and Gentile believers in Rome upon the return of Jewish believers into what would have become a largely Gentile church. James R. Edwards surmises that, "[i]n light of the probable conflicts between Jewish and Gentile Christians in Rome following the edict of Claudius . . . Paul clearly envisioned practical acts of giving as a way of overcoming the estrangement between Gentiles and Jews" (*Romans*, p. 296).

It is interesting that Paul's injunction to "practice hospitality" comes at the end of Romans 12:9-13. Perhaps the injunction does double duty here as the focus changes from loving the Christian community (12:9-13) to loving the world at large (12:14-21). As noted above, hospitality involves entertaining or welcoming strangers. The context of Romans 12:13 appears to apply the characteristic of hospitality in two different directions. The first direction is inward looking. As the family of God, Jews and Gentiles must be hospitable to one another, even if one group may seem like strangers to the other as a result of the recent expulsion of the Jews and rescinding of it in Rome. Secondly, in light of Romans 12:14-21, Christ-followers are also to pursue hospitality toward strangers in the world. Regarding this dual focus, hospitality within the church and hospitality toward strangers outside, the active pursuit of hospitality becomes a hallmark of the Christian faith. "The earthly conduct of the believing community," writes R. David Kaylor, "is to proclaim the message of God's salvation. Faith is proclaimed through the community of faith not as abstract truth stated in propositional terms but as lived truth expressed through the active life of the community" (*Paul's Covenant Community*, p. 195). In this light, hospitality demonstrated within the church and to those outside of it, even toward one's enemies (cf. 12:20), becomes, as Yong puts it, "the divinely appointed means of grace through which the world is drawn into the saving work of God in Christ" (*Hospitality and the Other*, p. 63). In light of all this, the apostle Paul appears to be calling the church at Rome to embrace hospitality as a way of life. Precisely, this way of hospitality can build unity among the church body while potentially open doors to strangers.

1 Timothy 3:2, 5:10; Titus 1:8

In the Pastoral Epistles, Paul writes to Timothy in Ephesus and Titus in Crete with instructions for church leaders and the church body in combating false teaching and in the behaviors that should mark Christians, which includes hospitality.

In 1 Timothy 3:2, Paul writes to Timothy regarding the characteristics which must be inherent in the life of bishops and deacons. Paul says these leaders must be "hospitable" (*philoxenon*). Literally, these leaders must live lives which embrace "the other." 1 Timothy 3:2 finds a parallel in Titus 1:8 where Paul mentions that elders "must be hospitable" (*philoxenon*). Hospitality is mentioned again in 1 Timothy 5:10, this time concerning the character of widows. In this context the statement "showing hospitality" appears as a *hapax legomenon* in the New Testament. The Greek word is *exenodochesan* which, according to George W. Knight, III, means "she has shown or given hospitality" (*The Pastoral Epistles*, p. 224). Knight points out that this word most likely carries the meaning of showing hospitality to traveling Christians, "especially those who come preaching or teaching" (p. 224). Interestingly, this statement regarding widows showing hospitality occurs directly before the statement about "washing the feet of the Lord's people." As we have already seen, footwashing was a common component of hospitality. It figured prominently in both accounts of Abraham and the three visitors and of Lot and his two visitors. There appears to be a direct connection between showing hospitality and footwashing. Hospitality characteristically expresses itself to both believers inside the local community and to the traveling stranger.

Commentators as a whole do not devote much attention to these references to hospitality in 1 Timothy or Titus. Nevertheless, the letters call all church leaders to conduct themselves in a manner which embraces the stranger, whether believer or nonbeliever, and to encourage others in the church to do likewise. As Donald Guthrie observes, "[Hospitality] would have particular point in the early church, since without the willing hospitality of Christian people expansion would have been seriously retarded" (*The Pastoral Epistles*, p. 92). Hospitality is as important to the mission of the church as it is to Christian character. It stands as a defining characteristic of those who claim to follow Christ.

Hebrews 13:2

Hebrews 13:2 also enjoins believers to practice hospitality: "Do not forget to show hospitality to strangers, for by so doing some have shown hospitality to angels without knowing it." The word translated "hospitality" in the first instance of this verse is *philoxenias* (lit., "a loving kindness to strangers").

F. F. Bruce (*The Epistle to the Hebrews*, p. 370) and Donald Hagner (*Hebrews*, p. 235) believe that this verse particularly has in mind traveling Christian workers much like 1 Timothy 5:10. If this is the case, this verse also points out the vital role hospitality should play in the spread of Christianity throughout the world. Hebrews 13:1 speaks to this issue in its exhortation to "keep on loving one another as brothers and sisters." Hospitality fleshes out love in concrete actions (Hagner, *Hebrews*, p. 234).

Another important aspect of Hebrews 13:2 relevant to this discussion pertains to the phrase, "for by doing so some have shown hospitality to angels without knowing it." This is obviously a reference to Abraham in Genesis 18, and perhaps to Lot in Genesis 19. In both of these instances, Abraham and Lot show hospitality to strangers who turn out to be angels, and in the case of Abraham one is Yahweh himself! Bruce points out that the author of Hebrews "is not necessarily encouraging his readers to expect that those whom they entertain will turn out to be supernatural beings traveling incognito; he is assuring them that some of their visitors will prove to be true messengers of God to them, bringing a greater blessing than they receive" (*Hebrews*, p. 371). This is also reminiscent of Jesus' instruction in the Parable of the Sheep and the Goats in Matthew 25:31-45. Jesus instructs his disciples that "Truly I tell you, whatever you did for one of the least of these brothers and sisters of mine, you did for me" (Matt. 25:40). The point is clear: Whenever a believer shows hospitality toward another, he or she is serving Jesus himself! And Matthew 25:45 reveals that the converse is also true: "Truly I tell you, whatever you did not do for one of the least of these, you did not do for me!"

Once again we see that hospitality is mentioned as a key characteristic for the Christian community and missional component for the spread of Christianity. Furthermore, showing hospitality toward others is tantamount to showing hospitality toward God himself!

1 Peter 4:9

First Peter 4:9 counsels the Christian readers to "offer hospitality (*philoxenoi*) to one another without grumbling." This verse is part of a larger context (including 1 Peter 4:7-11) pertaining to issues involving Christian living and character (Wayne Grudem, *1 Peter*, p. 172). This context fits with what we have seen so far regarding the other references to hospitality. For instance, a fascinating similarity exists between 1 Peter 4:9 and Hebrews 13:2. As noted above, Hebrews 13:1 mentions love as the root or basis of Christian character and living, with hospitality then appearing as an expression of it in Hebrews 13:2. Likewise, 1 Peter 4:8 states "Above all, love each other deeply, because love covers over a multitude of sins." As with the Hebrews passage, the injunction to "love each other" is followed by an admonition to "offer hospitality" in the next verse. "Earnest love, which seeks the good of others before one's own, finds practical expression in hospitality" (Grudem, *1 Peter*, p. 174). Ben Witherington supports this view when he points out that 1 Peter 4:9 "continues this interpretation" regarding the connection of love in 1 Peter 4:8 with hospitality (*Letters and Homilies for Hellenized Christians*, Vol 2, p.204). For the follower of Christ, the character of love seems inextricably linked with the act of hospitality.

So then, the context of 1 Peter 4:9 seems to dictate that genuine hospitality is deeply rooted in love. As such, it is a determining characteristic of the Christian community, and for our study, is "consistent with the rest of the New Testament." (Wayne Grudem, *1 Peter*, p. 174). The Great Commandment, love for God and others, can be witnessed in the church through hospitable behavior.

3 John 8

Much of the letter of 3 John has to do with the issue of hospitality, even though the word *philoxenia* is not utilized. *Hypolambanein* in 3 John 8 is translated as "hospitality" in the NIV and "support" in the NASB. The verse reads, "We ought therefore to show hospitality/support to such people so that we may work together for the truth." The broader context points the reader to the issue of hospitality.

The author of 3 John 5-8 praises Gaius for reaching out to Christian brothers and sisters, "even though they are strangers (*xenous*) to you" (3 John 5). Again, as with Hebrews 13:2 and 1 Peter 4:9, the broader context links hospitality to the prevailing characteristic of "love." Third John 6 states, "They have told the church about your love." According to 3 John 7 those receiving hospitality were missionaries: "It was for the sake of the Name that they went out." These missionaries received little, if no, help from the pagans among whom they ministered. Hence, the hospitality Gaius demonstrated toward them assisted in the furthering of God's mission (3 John 7-8; so Matt. 10:41-42).

That these "strangers" are depicted as missionaries is important for our study. The indication is that those receiving hospitality are already believers and, in fact, missionaries. John Stott explains, "'The brothers' and 'strangers' of verse 5 are no ordinary Christians who happen to be travelling from one city to another, but missionaries" (*The Letters of John*, p. 226). Marshall supports this understanding when he states that "missionaries are wholly dependent on God's people for their support" (p. 86), thus indicating that those to whom Gaius administered hospitality were missionaries. So then, in this epistle we can see that hospitality is vital to the mission of God through the church.

The other NT references to hospitality we have previously examined have similar points of comparison with 3 John 8. First, hospitality appears as an expression of Christian love (cf. 1 Cor. 13). Second, hospitality vitally supports missionaries and hence the furtherance of God's mission in this world. To show hospitality to traveling Christians is to participate in furthering the cause of Christ. And lastly, it appears that "strangers" (*xenos*) can apply to Christians as well as non-Christians, as is the case in 3 John 5.

So far our survey of NT occurrences of hospitality has proved fruitful, even demonstrating some correlations with hospitality within the OT. First, hospitality is to be an active part of every Christian community, since it is repeatedly connected to God's love. This should not come as a novel idea since God is love (1 John 4:8, 16) and functions as Divine Host in the Old Testament. In this light, godly Christian hospitality stems from and reflects the divine hospitality of Yahweh.

A second point relates to the role of hospitality in the mission of the church. As Christians travel the globe they become "strangers" to outside communities; however, Christian communities are called to support Christian missionaries because in doing so they support the great mission of God in this world. Believers are to entertain strangers and these strangers may be angels, Yahweh himself, missionaries or other believers and Christian travelers. Subsequently, Christians are to practice hospitality toward all who call on the name of Jesus Christ. It appears that the NT letters are silent as to entertaining non-believers in one's home. As Bruce Malina emphasizes, "Such hospitality to travelling Christians is both urged (see Rom. 12:13; 1 Pet. 4:9) and much practiced (e.g., Acts 17:7; 21:17; 28:7; Rom.16:23)" (*The Received Text and What It Cannot Do*, p. 185).

Thirdly, in the example of Paul on Malta in Acts 28 we see another correlation between the Old Testament and New Testament. In the accounts of Abraham and Lot, their giving of hospitality resulted in receiving something. For Abraham and Sarah they received the promise of a child. For Lot and his daughters they received safety from the destruction of Sodom and Gomorrah. For Paul, Acts 28 includes a reciprocal sense of hospitality. Publius shows hospitality to Paul and his companions, Paul heals Publius' father and others on the island, Publius and the islanders "honored in many ways" Paul and his companions which included new supplies and a new ship! Ultimately this display of hospitality resulted in the spreading of the gospel to the ends of the earth—namely Rome. The book of Acts ends with Paul in Rome boldly proclaiming the gospel of Jesus Christ. In the New Testament hospitality appears to play a major role in the furtherance of God's mission in the world.

THE PERSON OF PEACE IN THE MISSIONARY DISCOURSE - A PIVOTAL COMPONENT IN THE COMMUNITY CHURCH PLANTING (CCP) SYSTEM

As previously mentioned above, Bruce Bennett is a South African churchman and missionary with the Into Africa Project which is a ministry of One Mission Society. Bennett is also the developer of the Community Church Planting system which focuses upon planting reproducing churches. This church planting system relies heavily upon the related concepts of hospitality and the "person of peace" and has produced great fruit throughout Africa and other regions of the Majority World. Bennett proclaims that through this system over 35,000 churches have been planted reaching 3.9 million people. According to his Community Church Planting Manual, Bennett declares, "God's instruction to Kingdom workers is that they must seek a person of peace and work through the gracious act of hospitality" (Bruce Bennett, "Community Church Planting Manual," p. 65; unpublished, available at www.intoafricaproject.org). The "person of peace" passages in the Synoptic Gospels are Matthew 10:9-15; Mark 6:7-13; and Luke 9:1-6; 10:5-7, which we will now examine.

Matthew 10:9-15

Matthew 10:9-15 is part of a larger passage spanning Matthew 10:1-11:1. This chapter block of material is often referred to as Jesus' Missionary Discourse. In this passage, Jesus is instructing his disciples on matters related to self-care and provision while going out and proclaiming the gospel among the Jews. Included in this instruction is their reliance upon the hospitality of others (cf. 10:9-11). The means through which God will carry out this mission specifically involves receiving hospitality from strangers. Jesus says in Matthew 10:11, "Whatever town or village you enter, search there for some worthy person and stay at their house until you leave." The giving and reception of hospitality is stressed further in the following verse. If the missionary is brought into a home and the home is deserving, they are to "let [their] peace rest on it" (Matt. 10:13a). On the other hand, if the home is undeserving, they are to "let [their] peace return to [them]" (Matt. 10:13b). Matthew 10:14 clarifies the latter: "If anyone will not welcome you or listen to your words, leave that home or town and shake the dust off your feet."

The focus of this passage appears to deal more with worthy (*axios, axia*) persons over persons of peace. H. Douglas Buckwalter, a professor at Evangelical Seminary (Myerstown, Pa.), points this out in his proposed literary structure of Matthew 10. Buckwalter proposes a seven part chiastic structure for Matthew 10:1-11:1. According to his structure 10:5b-16 is paired with 10:32-42. Both points comprise the second and second-to-last points in the passage's overall structure:

B 10:5b-16 The people of Israel's reception or rejection ... of the disciples' preaching is described as the basis of their worthiness (*axios*, 10:11; *axia*, 10:13) or unworthiness *me...axia*, 10:13) [of Christ Jesus]—The audience's heart response is indicated by their outward behavior toward the disciples (in providing them housing).

B' 10:32-42 The people of Israel's reception ... or rejection ... of the disciples' preaching is prescribed as the basis of their worthiness or unworthiness (*ouk estin axios*, 3x, 10:37-38) of Jesus Christ—The audience's heart response is indicated by their outward behavior toward the disciples (in giving them a drink) .... (Buckwalter, class notes, Evangelical Seminary)

In these two passages, the emphasis is not on persons of peace but on the reception or rejection of the disciples' message, and thus whether the listeners are "worthy," which leads to peace if they are. Craig Keener falls within the same line of thinking: "The workers are 'worthy' . . . because they have made Jesus their first priority. . . . the question must be whether others would prove worthy to welcome them" (*A Commentary on the Gospel of Matthew*, p.

320). Stephen C. Barton adds further support when he states, "The identification of who is [worthy] is an important concern of Jesus' instruction in this very discourse (vv. 10, 11, 13)" (*Discipleship and Family Ties in Mark and Matthew*, p. 169). In the Matthean context, the disciples are looking for people who will receive their message. Hospitality shown to the disciples is a subsequent sign that the person has embraced the message preached.

Furthermore, the blessing of peace in this passage is based on whether the host receives or rejects the missionary disciple. If the disciples are received, then the peace of Christ "goes out and takes effect" within the household of the host (R. T. France, *The Gospel of Matthew*, p. 387.). If the disciples and their message are not received, then there is no effectual peace of Christ on that home or town. It "returns like an uncashed check" (p. 387).

When hospitality is refused, the disciples are to "shake the dust off their feet" as they leave that town (10:14). This "symbol of dissociation" (France, *The Gospel of Matthew*, p. 387) indicated that the disciples were to have nothing more to do with the home or town in which they visited. The result for the home or town would be worse than the judgment that befell Sodom and Gomorrah due to the fact that to reject Christ's disciple-missionaries is ultimately to reject Christ himself and his full revelation of the Father. It would appear, F. W. Beare argues, that there are rewards "that await those who receive Christ's messengers with honor or show kindness to his humblest followers" ("The Mission of the Disciples and the Mission Charge: Matthew 10 and Parallels," *Journal of Biblical Literature*, Vol. 89, 1970, p. 6). There are two possible rewards for those who demonstrate a spirit of hospitality toward Christ's disciples: (1) the peace of God (cf. Matt. 10:13) and (2) deep lasting relationship through induction into the community of Christ-followers. The disciples are worthy as carriers of the message of Christ while those who hear and receive their message are also worthy as is displayed in their practice of hospitality.

Mark 6:7-13

The Markan account is much shorter than that found in Matthew. Noticeably absent from the Markan account is any mention of worthy/worthiness or peace which is so prominent in Matthew's account. There are, however, similarities pertaining to issues of hospitality.

Mark similarly focuses on Jesus' disciple-missionaries trusting in God as they journey (R. Alan Cole, *Mark*, p. 169). The disciple-missionaries are not to be "self-sufficient," but rather reliant upon God for their needs (T. J. Rogers. "Shaking the Dust Off the Markan Missionary Discourse," *Journal for the Study of the New Testament*, 27.2, 2004, p. 178). As R. T. France observes, Christ's missionary disciples must "emphasize . . . loyalty to the kingdom of God [which] leaves no trace for a prior attachment to material security" (*The Gospel of Mark*, p. 250).

Mark makes similar reference to disciple-missionaries receiving hospitality ("enter a house"; Mark 6:10). T. J. Rogers asserts that for Mark, "there is no significant difference between refusing to offer hospitality and refusing to hear the gospel of Jesus Christ" ("Shaking the Dust Off the Markan Missionary Discourse," *Journal for the Study of the New Testament*, 27.2, 2004, p. 179). For instance, in Mark 6:11, Jesus declares, "If any place will not welcome you or listen to you, leave that place and shake the dust off your feet as a testimony against them." Notice that Jesus places the concepts of welcoming and hearing the gospel together, but mentions welcoming first. Hospitality is the focus "since it is mentioned first," and it is distinctly tied to hearing the gospel message (Rogers, p. 179).

Moreover, in examining the larger context in which Mark 6:7-13 falls, the preceding paragraph recounts Jesus' rejection by his own hometown in Nazareth (Mark 6:1-6). They were "amazed" at his teaching (6:2a). Yet, largely due to a lack of faith in him (6:6a), they ultimately "took offense at him" (6:3c). This episode sets up Jesus' Missionary Discourse in 6:7-13. Just as Jesus was rejected in his own hometown, the disciples should expect to be rejected as they carry the gospel message to the neighboring villages and towns. Rogers connects this to the theme of hospitality and Mark's apparent emphasis upon "shaking the dust from one's feet" as testimony to those who would refuse to give the disciples hospitality. He writes, "Had the twelve entered the town and been extended hospitality, as verse 10 directs, they would have been admitted to a house and their feet would have been washed according to custom. Thus, they would have been without dust on their feet" (Rogers, p. 182). Thus, Rogers suggests that just as with Matthew, the shorter Markan account relates hospitality to the idea that to receive Jesus' disciple-missionaries indicates that the host has received the gospel message, and thus Jesus himself; to refuse hospitality to one of Jesus' followers would indicate refusal of Jesus and all that knowing him entails.

Luke 9:1-6; 10:5-7

Luke's Gospel differs from Matthew and Mark in that he records Jesus sending out the disciples twice: the Twelve (9:1-6) and the Seventy-Two (10:5-7). Luke's account of the sending of the Twelve is shorter than Matthew's account and is also closer in wording to Mark's account than to Matthew. Nonetheless, it contains similar themes.

One of these themes is the instruction for the Twelve to travel light (9:3). In Luke, the missionary disciples are not permitted to take anything, not even a staff ("Take nothing for the journey"). In Mark's account the disciples were at least permitted a staff (Mark 6:8; "Take nothing for the journey except a staff"). Matthew's account does not permit money, bag, extra shirt or sandals, or a staff (Matt. 10:9-10). However, the overall point found in all three Synoptic Gospels is that Jesus' disciple-missionaries are to live a life that demonstrates complete trust and reliance upon the Father in their dependence on others to provide for their essential needs (Walter L. Leifeld, *Luke*, p. 124 and Leon Morris, Luke, p. 179).

Providing hospitality is also a major component of Luke's account. At first glance, however, Mark and Matthew's account significantly differ from Luke's portrayal. Mark brings together two concepts: 1) welcoming the missionary and 2) listening to the missionary. For Mark, to welcome the missionary is to welcome the message the missionary brings (Mark 6:11). The same two concepts appear in Matthew as well (Matt. 10:14). Luke, however, does not mention the listening. According to Luke 9:5, Jesus states, "If people do not welcome you, leave their town and shake the dust off your feet as a testimony against them." While the message is not directly connected to the issue of giving or withholding hospitality to missionary disciples, Luke's account still stresses the message itself. Jesus "sent them out to proclaim the kingdom of God" (9:2); "they went out and went from village to village, proclaiming the good news" (9:6). The word "proclaim" acts as an *inclusio* of sorts, emphasizing the importance of the message carried to the villages by the disciples.

What is more, as with Matthew and Mark, Luke records the counsel Jesus gives his disciples regarding the houses or towns who reject their message. The visual indicating judgment is again related to the lack of offered hospitality—"shake the dust off your feet as a testimony against them."

Luke 10:5-7 is part of a larger passage encompassing Luke 10:1-25 which begins with Jesus sending out the 72 disciples, followed by the teaching he had given them before sending them out. We will not discuss the entire passage in detail except once again to note several similarities between Matthew 10:9-15, Mark 6:7-13, Luke 9:1-6, and this passage. Reference is made to the disciples trusting in God for the journey (10:4), receiving hospitality (10:8), and dealing with rejection and the lack of hospitality (10:10-15). Of more immediate relevance to our study, however, is 10:5-7.

Luke 10:6 refers to a "person of peace," a concept absent in the other Synoptic passages. Jesus says, "If someone who promotes peace is there, your peace will rest on them; if not, it will return to you." Literally, "someone who promotes peace" is *huios eirenes,* "son of peace." This is different from Matthew, Mark and Luke 9:1-6. Mark and Luke 9:1-6 do not mention "peace," and Matthew mentions it in reference to the worthiness of the host. Specifically, those who receive the message of the disciples, thus receiving the missionaries, receive peace (Matt. 10:13). But the peace passes from the missionary to the host, not from the host to the missionary. John Koenig, in summarizing the relationship between missionary activity and hospitality in Luke-Acts, states, "The very structure of Luke's work witnesses to a conviction on his part that some deep link exists between the verbal content of God's good news and its historical embodiment in boundary situations involving guests and hosts. . . . For Luke, partnership with strangers becomes a natural feature of mission" (*New Testament Hospitality*, p. 86-87). This partnership with strangers is carried out in the role and characteristic of hospitality within the larger church body.

The Missionary Discourse of the Synoptic Gospels bears some similarities to the Old Testament and New Testament Epistle passages we examined. For instance, in Matthew, Mark, and Luke we saw that God's missionary disciples are called to a life of full trust and reliance upon God. God the Father will provide for the needs of his children as they go about engaging in his mission work. This harkens back to God providing abundantly in the Garden for Adam and Eve and for the needs of Israel in their wilderness wanderings. The theme of hospitality running through the Missionary Discourse ultimately runs through the mission of God itself.

In conjunction with the Epistles, hospitality in the Missionary Discourse is also the reliance of missionary disciples upon other believers for hospitality and assistance in furthering the mission of God. As Walter L. Leifeld states, "Servants of Christ should go forth, not seeking support from unbelievers, but trusting God completely to supply their needs through his people" (*Luke*, p. 124). Once again it seems that hospitality among the larger church body is vital to the global Missio Dei.

Lastly, the only apparent reference to a "person of peace" as defined by Bruce Bennett is found in Luke 10:5-7. Mark and Luke 9:1-6 make no mention of peace or even worth/worthiness. Matthew does speak of worth/worthiness as a necessary quality of the hosts who receive the missionary disciples. As such, these hosts receive peace from their guest missionaries.

HOSPITALITY AND THE MINISTRY OF JESUS

Throughout his earthly career, Jesus played the role of both guest and host. Hospitality, the receiving of the other, played a vital part. We can see this in how he lived while walking this earth and in the life of the early church which emulated him in this respect.

Jesus Welcoming the Other in His Ministry

Jesus consistently welcomed the "other," the stranger and the outcast throughout his earthly ministry. Whether it was sitting at a table sharing a meal with tax collectors and "sinners" (Matt. 9:10-11) or reaching out to a Samaritan woman at a well by asking her for a drink (John 4), Jesus' ministry revolved around embracing the "other." Jesus' manner of ministry placed him uniquely in the role of guest and host. Amos Yong expounds on this aspect of Christ's ministry:

> Throughout his public ministry, Jesus as the recipient of hospitality is at the same time the one who heralds and person- ifies the redemptive hospitality of God. He is the "journeying prophet" of the Spirit who eats at the tables of others but at the same time proclaims and brings to pass the eschatological banquet of God for all those who are willing to receive it (*Hos- pitality and the Other*, p. 102).

Hospitality carries an inherent risk. When God created the world and placed humanity in the Garden of Eden there was risk. In making humanity free, free to choose and free to accept or reject his divine hospitality, God took a gamble. He took another gamble, it would appear, through the Incarnation. Sending his Son, the Savior of the world, in the flesh of a baby was risky. This risk is pointed out by the author of the Fourth Gospel. John 1:10-12 poignantly displays the dichotomy involved in this risk. These verses declare, "He was in the world, and though the world was made through him, the world did not recognize him. He came to that which was his own, but his own did not receive him." This is the risk of hospitality, the risk of rejection. As theologian Miroslav

Volf expounds, "Without a certain kind of 'gamble'—a gamble on account of grace—truly human life would be impossible" (*Exclusion and Embrace*, p. 147). In rejecting the hospitality of God one cuts himself off from the abundant blessings of the Divine Host.

Volf continues:

> The risk [of embrace] follows both from nonsymmetricity and systematic underdetermination. I open my arms, make a movement of the self toward the other, the enemy, and do not know whether my action will be misunderstood, despised, even violated or whether my action will be appreciated, supported, and reciprocated. I can become a victim or a savior—possibly both (*Exclusion and Embrace*, p. 147).

On the other hand, those who do receive the hospitality of God through Jesus Christ find full identity and purpose. John 1:12 points this out: "Yet to all who did receive him, to those who believed in his name, he gave the right to become children of God." Hospitality is risky because it does not force anything on the "other." Hospitality is an open invitation to receive freely from the host and thus be transformed in some manner or fashion. In this instance, grace, which is a gamble, is witnessed in the character and nature of Jesus Christ. As we saw earlier in regard to teaching on New Testament hospitality, this must also be characteristic of Jesus' disciples.

Jesus as the "Other" . . . and Seeing Ourselves as the "Other"

Jesus not only embraced the strangers and outcasts in his midst, but he also embraced his role as "other." One way this can be seen is through Jesus' role as Christ or Messiah. Much of Jewish culture of Jesus' day envisioned a Messianic deliverer who would act as political savior to the nation of Israel. This, however, was not the way in which Jesus lived or conducted his ministry. In fact, John 6:15 records that when a crowd attempted to make him king by force, he fled to a place of solitude.

Another aspect of Jesus' otherness is revealed in his servant attitude. Throughout the Gospel records, Jesus regularly instructs his disciples to be servant-leaders. For example, Jesus tells them that the greatest among them should be as those who serve (cf. Luke 22:25-27, Matt. 20:26-28). Jesus even points himself out as the example: "But I am among you as one who serves" (Luke 22:27b). H. Douglas Buckwalter surmises that this is the overarching theme of Luke's writings:

> To sum up my proposal concerning a primary literary objective of Luke: he writes to show his readers how Jesus' life stands as the ethical model for Christian living and how the early church has imaged his likeness in their own life and witness. According to Luke, the corollary to the Lord Jesus' servanthood is Christian discipleship (*The Character and Purpose of Luke's Christology*, p. 281).

This lines up with what we have seen thus far concerning the role of hospitality in the mission of God. We have seen that hospitality is to be a characteristic of Jesus' disciples and, therefore, by default a characteristic of the church at large. Welcoming others stands as a biblical hallmark of the faith.

This servanthood aspect of embracing otherness reflects, in Thomas W. Ogletree's words, "reversals in the relational order" (Hospitality to the Stranger, p. 4). Elizabeth Newman also echoes this point, observing that, "The faithful practice of hospitality requires that we see ourselves as both guests, receiving from the other, and hosts, offering ourselves to the other. Such hospitality acknowledges that truth might come from 'strange' quarters" (*Untamed Hospitality*, p. 144).

Again, Ogletree expounds upon this idea:

> To offer hospitality to a stranger is to welcome something new, unfamiliar, and unknown into our life-world. On the one hand, hospitality requires a recognition of the stranger's vulnerability in an alien social world. Strangers need shelter and sustenance in their travels, especially when they are moving through a hostile environment. On the other hand, hospitality designates occasions of potential discovery which can open up our narrow, provincial worlds. Strangers have stories to tell

which we have never heard before, stories which can direct our seeing and stimulate our imaginations. The stories invite us to view the world from a novel perspective. They display the finitude and relativity of our own orientation and meaning (*Hospitality to the Stranger*, pp. 2-3).

Ogletree's statement is illustrated in the life of Christ. For those who were open to receiving him would often discover in the process not only Jesus' true identity but subsequently their own as well (cf. Luke 8:48). Quite often, after an encounter with Christ, the person transformed through it would go and tell others about Jesus, even inviting them to come and see him for themselves (cf. John 4:28-30; Mark 5:20). In embracing the other and his own otherness, Jesus gave his followers the litmus test for discipleship. His followers must also embrace others and their own sense of otherness (i.e., living according to Jesus' way and not the world's) in this world (cf. Phil. 2:1-11).

Jesus exhibited throughout his earthly ministry a lifestyle that embraced both the "other" (the stranger) and his own "otherness." For disciples, "otherness" connotes living in the present world as "foreigners" and "exiles" (cf. 1 Peter 2:10-12). This "relational reversal" that guided Jesus in his ministry must also be evident in the life of his disciples. Hospitality appears as a defining mark or characteristic of discipleship and a vital aspect to the life of the church. However, hospitality is inherently risky, a "gamble." It is risky because the host is not guaranteed a positive response from the guest. Nevertheless, the risky venture of the Incarnation is the highest example of hospitality and servanthood that Christ's followers must emulate through mission in the world.

CHAPTER 5:

THE "PERSON OF PEACE" IN MODERN MISSION MOVEMENTS

Modern church multiplication movements (CMM) utilize hospitality coupled with the "person of peace" as crucial elements of their systems of producing more churches. For this study, as introduced earlier (see p. 5), we will specifically examine the system utilized by Bruce Bennett of South Africa.

BRUCE BENNETT AND THE COMMUNITY CHURCH PLANTING MOVEMENT

In his "Community Church Planting" manual, Bruce Bennett defines the "person of peace" as follows:

> A person of peace is someone who, even though they are not a believer, is open to listening and finding out more about Jesus. They are people that the Spirit of God has been preparing to play strategic roles in facilitating the expansion of the Kingdom of God" (p. 85).

Bennett finds an example of a "person of peace" in Zacchaeus (cf. Luke 19:1-10). According to Bennett, Zacchaeus was "God's chosen vessel; an influential witness to God's transforming grace long after Jesus had left" Jericho (p. 85). Bennett believes "Zacchaeus was looking for Jesus. Jesus was looking for Zacchaeus. Jesus sends us to find people of peace whom God has prepared. [People of peace] are looking for us. We must look for them. We are bound to find each other" (p. 85). According to Bennett this notion of the "person of peace" is the crucial component to church multiplication.

In the manual, Bennett also outlines three components which are found in a "person of peace" (p. 90): First, a "person of peace" is "receptive to the Gospel because of a prior work of the Holy Spirit in their lives." Second, they are "reputable and [have] influence in their community." And finally, he or she "refers God's workers to others and has influence in opening the community to the Gospel." These characteristics are found in such biblical examples as the Samaritan woman (John 4:1-42), Andrew (John 1:40-42), the lame man at the Beautiful Gate (Acts 3:1-11), Aeneas (Acts 9:32-35), Cornelius (Acts 10), Sergius Paulus (Acts 13:1-12), Saul at his conversion (Acts 9:1-22), Lydia (Acts 16:11-15), the jailer (Acts 16:25-34), and Zacchaeus (Luke 19:1-10).

Others have similarly pointed to the importance of the "person of peace" within church planting movements (CPM) and church multiplication movements (CMM). David Garrison, whose view of the "person of peace" is nearly identical to that of Bennett, has studied CMMs around the globe and attests to the importance of the "person of peace":

> Several of the Church Planting Movements we've examined attest to the missionary method of sending church planters into villages in search of God's "person of peace," that individual already chosen by God to receive the Gospel message. Their motivation is to adhere to the model established by Jesus. When Jesus first dispatched his disciples as missionaries, he sent them out two-by-two and commanded them to enter every village in search of the "man of peace" who would welcome them and their message (*Church Planting Movements*, p. 211).

Another example can be found in the work of Australia's Steve Addison. Addison, like Garrison, is a student of the CMM. He points out that early Christianity appears to have spread rapidly through social networks of friends and relatives (*Movements that Change the World*, p. 74). Concerning the "person of peace," Addison writes:

Jesus moved from village to village looking for responsive people who would take the good news into the world of their relationships. He built long-term relationships with his disciples, but he had a harvest model of evangelism. Always on the move, he scattered the seed of the Gospel broadly and then watched it multiply through others . . . He sent out his disciples with the instructions to look for a "person of peace" wherever they went—a well-known person of the community who was receptive to the messengers and the message. The disciples on mission had no relational contacts of their own; the person of peace became the bridge into the community's social networks [as in Luke 10] (*Movements that Change the World*, p. 81).

As with Garrison, Addison's definition of a "person of peace" is similar to Bennett's definition. For all three men, "the key for the spread of the gospel is contagious relationships" (Addison, *Movements that Change the World*, p. 82) most notably through the "person of peace."

Perhaps another example of how the "person of peace" has been utilized in missions can be seen in the work of Vincent J. Donovan, who evangelized among the Masai people in Tanzania. Donovan shares how he taught the Masai by involving a member of the local Masai community. Essentially, Donovan utilized a "person of peace." He shares the following account:

By the time I started the second wave of evangelization among new villages, I had developed a different way of carrying on the dialogue with the Masai. I would look for someone in the very first meeting with a new people, someone who seemed to understand the message better than the others. At the end of the meeting, when the crowd dispersed, I would ask that person to remain. I would go over what he had covered in the meeting, and ask him if, at the beginning of the next meeting, he could refresh everyone's memory as to what we had talked about. When he had finished doing this at the next meeting, I would take over and continue on with new things. In some places it was very difficult, if not impossible, to find such a person. In some places the system worked very well, and in such places, after many meetings, we had a pagan in the group who, unknown to himself, was a catechist in the making (*Christianity Rediscovered*, p. 84).

While Donovan's example among the Masai people may differ in some ways from the "person of peace" of the other models, it nonetheless provides a practical example of utilizing a relational insider within a community to help spread the gospel message. In essence, Donovan used a "person of peace."

The "person of peace" appears to be a well-established missionary method which has resulted in the rapid spread of the gospel and response to it throughout the Majority World. But before moving on, we must briefly address an issue related to the "person of peace"—the focus on the rapid spread of the gospel within these movements.

RAPID EXPANSION

A topic often appearing in discussions of CPMs and CMMs is the rapid spread or rapid growth of these movements. Spontaneous and rapid growth is seemingly expected.

Bennett writes, "The urgency of the hour calls for an exponential church planting model that will saturate communities" ("Community Church Planting" manual, p. 9). On the nature of rapid church growth, Garrison states, "Today's Western Christians who have seen only individual commitments to Christ may have trouble understanding this spontaneous and sweeping response to the Gospel, but it was common in the New Testament world. And it is common in today's Church Planting Movements" (*Church Planting Movements*, p. 215). And in *Movements that Change the World*, Addison devotes a whole chapter to this topic, titled "Rapid Mobilization."

This discussion on the spontaneous and rapid expansion of movements can most likely be traced back to the work of Roland Allen. Allen was an Anglican missionary to China from 1895 to 1903 and is best known for his book, The Spontaneous Expansion of the Church. On this subject, he wrote, "This was not a peculiar note of the apostolic age, a sign of amazing inspiration and power of apostolic preaching and example: for centuries the Christian Church continued to expand by its own inherent grace, and threw up an unceasing supply of missionaries without any direct exhortation" (p. 6).

Allen defines spontaneous expansion as follows:

> I mean the expansion which follows the unexhorted and unorganized activity of the individual members of the Church explaining to others the Gospel which they have found for themselves; I mean the expansion which follows the irresistible attraction of the Christian Church for men who see its ordered life, and are drawn to it by desire to discover the secret life which they instinctively desire to share; I mean also the expansion of the Church by the addition of new churches (*The Spontaneous Expansion of the Church*, p. 7).

According to this definition from Allen, we see can the important role that relational networks appear to play in such growth. Notice how Allen puts it: "explaining to others" who "instinctively desire to share."

This leads us to a couple of important questions: Can one expect spontaneous growth or even search for such growth? Are there dangers in doing so? Steve Smith and Ying Kai, coauthors of *T4T: A Discipleship Re-Revolution*, believe this expectation is a vital part of CMMs:

There may be hardened people groups, but in every one there are harvestable individuals! You may have to work harder to find the harvest but it is there. In some contexts, perhaps one out of every ten or twenty lost people is a prepared "person of peace" (Luke 10:6), while in other contexts it could be one out of a hundred or thousand. You just have to work harder to find the first persons of peace (p. 83).

This approach seems a bit different from the "spontaneous" approach, which allows the Holy Spirit to guide the "person of peace" procedure.

From another perspective, let us briefly examine a recent article by Kyle Faircloth, a missionary in Asia, who addresses the issue of expected rapid growth. Faircloth argues that the focus on rapid growth may have unintended consequences. For example, Faircloth believes "when rapidity is the key ingredient for strategy, even the biblical meanings risk reduction" ("Searching for the Indigenous Method," *Evangelical Missions Quarterly*, 48.4, October 2012, p. 398). According to Faircloth, there is an inherent danger when missions/missionaries preach strategy over Scripture, even if the strategy is developed from Scripture. Furthermore, Faircloth points out that "one common misconception in CPM strategy is that the indigenous method equals rapid multiplication" (p. 399). While it has been true that the gospel spreads through social networks and pre-existing relationships, that is still no guarantee for rapid growth.

Another danger that Faircloth addresses is that the "demand for a CPM puts unnecessary pressure on church planters to equivocate these principles" (p. 399). The call of rapid replication of movements, churches, and also the strategies which must accompany these systems can become a burden to church planters depending on context. As a possible corrective, Faircloth argues, "Perhaps the answer is not to alter the strategy to be rapid, but to be biblical. To identify 'slow' as the problem means even biblical principles may be abridged if they slow down the process. At the same time we must not vilify the concept of 'rapid' in itself" (p. 400-401). I believe this is apparent when we look at hospitality in the Scripture. As we have already witnessed, hospitality is demonstrated as a characteristic of disciples and thus the larger church body. Hospitality was also associated with God's missionary movement, but nowhere did we see any notion of this emphasis on rapid growth as Faircloth rightly notes.

Another possible area we witness this "rapid" mindset at work deals with the expression "person of peace." According to the definitions above, the general consensus is that the "person of peace" is a non-believer. However, in light of the New Testament evidence we have examined, the "person of peace" could be either a non-believer or a believer who shows hospitality to a missionary and supports God's mission. Furthermore, as Fairchild articulates, "the concept of 'rapid' must be informed not by CPM strategy, but by the urgency bound up in the heart of God. God is not oblivious to the urgency of his mission" (p. 401). For the believer it is God who is to be the focus, not rapid reproduction or expansion.

As a case-in-point, prior to Donovan's work, many believed that the Masai were an unreachable, closed-off people group. This was most likely the result of failed missionary strategy. Donovan, however, took it upon himself to go out to the Masai and meet with the community once a week and give them nothing but the unencumbered gospel of Jesus Christ. This process took an entire year and the result was not always positive (Donovan, *Christianity Rediscovered*, p. 81). Not all of the Masai "kraals" Donovan visited accepted the message of Jesus Christ. However, by the time he returned to the United States, one could claim that the Masai were reached due to the number of "kraals" that accepted the message and carried it to others.

The words of Anthony J. Gittins are germane to this discussion:

> We are sent, and mission is not undertaken on our own terms: God's Spirit (Acts 16:6) and the local people have something to contribute. We are sent, moreover, to be in relation (communio, koinonia) with people who are not merely receptive ears and willing re-actors, but speakers of words of life and conversations, capable initiators themselves, and ultimately agents under God, of our own ongoing conversion ("Beyond Hospitality? The Missionary Status and Role Revisited," *Currents in Theology and Mission*, 21.3, June 1994, p. 166).

The focus on rapid growth movements and strategies is not inherently wrong; however, if unchecked they could potentiality lead to the neglect of the reciprocal nature inherent in the hospitable mission of God. In the simple words of Kosuke Koyama, "Mission is 'extending hospitality to strangers'" ("Extend Hospitality to Strangers—A Missiology of Theologia Crucis," *International*

Review of Mission, 82.327, July-October 1993, p. 167). Cultivating hospitality appears to be a crux in carrying out the Mission Dei.

"Will it work here?"—The Issue of Contextualization for the Western Church

Church multiplication movements, such as Bruce Bennett's, are seemingly flourishing throughout the Majority World. As mentioned above, Bennett's CPM has seen over 3.9 million members and over 35,000 churches planted in about a decade. The majority of these are found in Africa and Asia. Glaringly absent is the American church. Why? What is found in the Majority World that would seem to allow for such rapid and spontaneous growth? What would it take to see a CPM or CMM at work in America? Although America has shifted from modernity to post-modernity, it remains heavily influenced by the effects of modernity. This, as we will see, must be understood if the American church is to utilize the twin concepts of hospitality and the "person of peace" in hopes of revitalizing what appears to be a church with declining influence in its own culture.

Time and Hospitality

One area that must be addressed involves the nature of time as it relates to hospitality. By its nature, hospitality is meant to be short-term and temporary. In light of this, there must be some sort of transition from the short-term nature of hospitality to a longer maturing relationship.

The issue of time itself, however, has been heavily influenced by modernity. Paul G. Hiebert addresses this when he argues that the clock has been one of the most influential inventions of the modern age: "The clock has made us into timekeepers, then time savers, now time-servers" (*Transforming Worldviews*, p. 52). As a result, Westerners have a completely different concept of time. One way this could negatively affect hospitality and CPMs is related to punctuality. In light of Westerners being "time-servers," time is a limited commodity that can only be used wisely and given to a select group of people. One result is that Westerners can view themselves as superior to the Majority World due to the differing concepts of time. The non-American may, for example, be viewed as lazy according to the American idea of time.

When I visited Kenya in 2012, our African brothers and sisters referred to the West's emphasis on time with the phrase "the power of the watch." Ironically, many in America do not even have time for family or close friends anymore, let alone any time for hospitality and welcoming the "other." Helpful here is Jonathan Bonk's theology of interruptions. Bonk provides a corrective to the western church with this reminder:

> Truly Christian mission is never ethereal or speculative. It is always incarnational, addressing real human beings at the point of their personal circumstances, whatever the larger context over which neither we nor they have any control. Effective mission can never be merely the byproduct of strategizing and action, but has always been carried out by passionate believers, who cannot help but speak those things they have seen and heard (*Thinking Small*, p. 11).

Because mission involves real people and personal circumstances, it cannot, by nature, be something that is neat, orderly, and scheduled according to the likes of modernity.

INDIVIDUALISM AND HOSPITALITY

Another aspect of modernity is its focus on individualism. Hiebert, in quoting Peter Berger, writes, "It has been suggested that the theme of individual autonomy is perhaps the most important theme in the worldview of modernity" (*Transforming Worldviews*, p. 168). Hiebert then points out potential results of individualism when he writes, "The price of individualism and freedom is a lack of strong, permanent personal relationships and security. The autonomous person is a person alone, never in a community greater than he or she. Social groups are fluid and less important than the individual" (p. 171). In a world of seven billion people and the social media craze people still seem to be more alone and isolated than ever, even with hundreds or thousands of Facebook "friends."

If Hiebert is correct that individualism is the major theme of the Western modern worldview, individualism then often produces a lack of hospitality and transforming relationships within the greater community, and especially within the church. No room is left for welcoming the stranger or the "other" because, similar to the issue of time, the focus is inward rather than outward. The mission of God, and subsequently the church, must possess elements of both the inward and the outward. This includes the role and nature of hospitality. In the final analysis, if this is neglected, one is left with quasi-community which only has the appearance of mutuality and benefit for others, and there is little room for hospitality.

ENGINEERING MENTALITY AND HOSPITALITY

Another controlling factor of Western thought and culture is the "engineering mentality." Hiebert reveals the heart of this mindset when he writes:

> Another way in which the church in the West has been shaped by modernity can be seen in its focus on tasks and techniques, rather than on community and relationships. Being the church and doing missions are tasks that we associate with our abilities to make things happen and to take control. The result is an engineering mentality. In churches business meetings focus on finding the right techniques to solve the problems of the church. In missions, church planting and growth can be done well if the right techniques are found through quantitative data, analysis, and testing of various methods (*Transforming Worldviews*, p. 167; emphasis mine).

In relation to hospitality, Elizabeth Newman supports Hiebert's view: "One of the common assumptions about hospitality is that it is primarily about doing something and getting certain results" (*Untamed Hospitality*, p. 180). In light of this "engineering mentality," hospitality is only deemed valuable if there is a payoff of some sort. If the host is not receiving something deemed valuable from the guest such as money, time or results, then it is viewed as wasteful. True hospitality, however, is built around the opposite view. The host spending time and resources on behalf of the guest was at one time seen as a sacred practice. Now, in the West it no longer appears to be sacred or valuable unless something of equal or greater value is given in return. We can even see individualism affecting this mindset by what appears to by the accompanying attitude "what's in it for me?"

Time, coupled with individualism and the "engineering mentality," must be reversed to some degree if hospitality is to once again play a vital role in the life of the western church. It seems that Bennett and others are dangerously close to the "engineering mentality," especially in regard to their teaching on the "person of peace" as the pivotal role in CPMs and CMMs. The focus on the "person of peace" rather than developing long-term healthy relationships is a mistake. For example, I once spoke with a mission director from America who implemented Bennett's Village Church Planting (VCP) system in an area of Africa. This particular denomination witnessed growth in this geographical area; however, another denomination became involved with these African churches and offered to pay their pastors. As a result, these churches broke with one denomination and joined another over the issue of paid pastors—money! I believe this instance is an example of what could happen if the mission of the church is approached from the American mindsets of time, individualism and the engineering mentality. Ultimately, there is no substitute for building deep and lasting relationships through which hospitality can be a catalyst.

CONTROL AND HOSPITALITY

Another factor which is similar to the "engineering mentality" involves the Westerner's need for control. "At the heart of modernity," writes Paul Hiebert, "is the quest for order and control and the preoccupation with the elimination or reduction of forms of disorder through the engineering and management of orderliness in modern forms of life" (*Transforming Worldviews*, p. 158). One way this may be a factor is if hospitality and the "person of peace" concept become nothing more than a system of operation or mechanized approach to outreach that is rooted in a need for control and management. However, as both Scripture and history point out, control is an apparent illusion for humanity. Humanity cannot control church growth. As Jonathan Bonk declares, "Christian mission in the twenty-first century will continue to be done by God's people, in God's way, since this is God's world. And God has always used 'ordinary' individuals whose identification with Christ makes it impossible for them to remain silent or to sit still within contexts over which neither they nor their listeners have any control" (*Thinking Small*, pp. 12-13). Going back nearly a century, Rolland Allen writes:

> We fear [spontaneous expansion] because we feel that it is something that we cannot control. And that is true. We can neither induce nor control spontaneous expansion whether we look on it as the work of the individual or of the church, simply because it is spontaneous . . . and spontaneous activity is a movement of the Spirit in the individual and in the Church, and we cannot control the Spirit (*Spontaneous Expansion*, p. 12).

According to Scripture, humanity "plants" and "waters" the seed; however, it is God who causes the growth (1 Cor. 3:6). Furthermore, God was the cause of the rapid and spontaneous growth of the early church (cf. Acts 2:47). Spontaneous growth, no matter how deeply desired, cannot be fabricated nor controlled through mechanistic means. As pointed out above, it is always risky because the outcome cannot be known beforehand. Hospitality is still a doorway, however, for growth as one can witness in CPMs and CMMs such as Bennett's and others throughout the Majority World.

TRANSITION AND HOSPITALITY

A final issue the West must address involves a needed transition which must take place in order to form deep and lasting community. By its very nature, hospitality is short-term. Walter Vogels writes ". . . but hospitality was never an offer of permanent residence. The longest stay attested in the biblical stories is four nights, and this was already an extended stay (Judges 19:4-9). If a guest stayed longer, he would become a burden to the host; conversely, if the host kept the guest longer, this could be interpreted as hostility (Gen. 24:32, 54-61)" ("Hospitality in Biblical Perspective," *Liturgical Ministry*, vol. 11, fall 2002, p. 166). In the account of Abraham's servant and Rebekah from Genesis 24, as noted above, Laban borders on the edge of hostility by attempting to keep the servant, and thus Rebekah, longer than necessary. To this issue Christine Pohl adds, "Some of the most difficult questions about boundaries arise not so much in connection with hospitality as with membership in the community. Long-term guest status is disempowering, and in most communities, if the guest stays on, there is eventually a change in role" (*Making Room*, p. 140). These boundaries within hospitality are vital to the relationship, dignity, and overall health of the parties involved.

Furthermore, while hospitality can act as a doorway there must be a transition within the role of guest and host that forms a longer-lasting relationship. This relationship transitions beyond the initial moment of hospitality. As we saw above in our examination of the theme of hospitality in the Old Testament, long-term relationship development appears to be at the heart of the hospitality Yahweh demonstrated to his people. Christopher Heuertz and Christine Pohl issue a similar reminder: "We've learned that short-term models of mission—whether in the form of week-long mission trips or one or two-year commitments to serve—might be workable in certain situations, but in ministry with the most vulnerable people, a community has to be prepared to stay. It takes years to build the kind of relationships that result in transformation" (*Friendship at the Margins*, p. 28). The same idea must guide this transition today, if the western church is to build true and lasting community.

The ministry of Ahmed Ali Haile illustrates how the short-term nature of hospitality can be used effectively for long-term outcomes. Haile, a Somali-born Muslim who converted to Christianity, utilized hospitality as a major component within his role as peacemaker in the war-torn nation of Somalia. Haile shares about a meeting he had with four *ugas*, or kings, of different Somali clans. The meeting involved a shared meal together, which Haile describes:

> That evening was a defining moment. The symbolic significance of eating together in my home was tremendous; it meant from then on I was accepted within my clan system and, by extension, within the entire Somali system. I was again an insider. However, being included involves much more than just a meal together. Relationships had to be cultivated. We did that. Every week ten to twenty elders from my clan would come to our home for discussions and food. Martha oversaw the cooking. We ate and fellowshipped and conversed vigorously together. In that way our covenant of peace was renewed each week (*Teatime in Mogadishu*, p. 79).

To be sure, hospitality is risky and often uncontrollable. For Haile, it meant eventually losing a leg to a grenade at the hands of another who disagreed with his peacemaking work. Hospitality is not always clean and neat but more often than not is messy as people are pulled into the lives of others. As Haile's wife, Martha Jean, attests, "Not to be confused with entertaining, hospitality meant welcoming people into our hearts and home. As our children noted, this was not always convenient" (*Teatime in Mogadishu*, p. 129). The transition from short-term to long-term relations can be difficult but is necessary for building true and lasting community especially within the church. In order for this kind of community to transpire the host and guest must be vulnerable toward one another.

IDENTITY AND HOSPITALITY

At the core of this discussion is the issue of identity. Amos Yong puts it this way: "Given the interrelationship between beliefs and practices . . . being the church—the body of Christ—is defined not only by who we are but also by what we do. The latter involves bearing witness to Christ, whose disciples we are. Hence . . . , there is no denying this missionary aspect of our ecclesial identity" (*Hospitality and the Other*, p. 130). The Missio Dei is a major part of the

Church's identity. If we are correct in stating that God is hospitable by nature and the focus of his hospitality is long-term relationship, then it is true to say that, in Yong's words, "Christian mission is nothing more or less than our participation in the hospitality of God" (p. 131). In addition, as Yong states, "Evangelization is in the scheme of things nothing more or less than our having experienced God's redemptive hospitality and our inviting others to experience the same" (p. 131). Essentially, as others have pointed out, disciples of Jesus are like beggars telling other beggars where to find bread.

In this light, it would appear that the root issue for the American church is the need for recovery of this missional identity grounded in the redemptive hospitality of Yahweh himself. The church is both guest and host in the world. We are guest of God's divine hospitality and hosts to the "others" in this world.

As the western church recovers this missional identity rooted in hospitality, I suggest that the transition which must take place will ultimately be found in the "family of God." The Scriptures repeatedly show the divine hospitality of God at work. The consummate result for those who receive this divine hospitality is a change of identity and lasting relationship. This can be summed up in the words of John 1:12: "Yet to all who did receive him, to those who believed in his name, he gave the right to become children of God." God has poignantly demonstrated the extent of his hospitality in giving his very own Son (John 3:16-17). In order to receive this great gift of abundant hospitality, reflects Kimberly D. Booser, "a person must believe (i.e., embrace and follow) Jesus Christ; he cannot become a child of God by his own effort. It is God who has enabled him to become his child," a part of his family ("The Literary Structure of John 1:1-18," *Evangelical Journal*, 16.1, spring 1998, p. 27-28). For one to receive the hospitality of God is to become a member of God's household through Jesus Christ.

Regarding praxis, missiologist Dana L. Robert points out that the Christian home is "almost completely ignored . . . [in] mission theory today" ("What Happened to the Christian Home? The Missing Component of Mission Theory," *Missiology*, vol. 33, 2005, p. 327). Robert further contends that the primary reason this aspect is largely ignored is because "[m]ost church leaders consider the 'real' mission work to be male-driven church planting and theological education, rather than such 'auxiliary' ministries such as hospitality and home visitation" (p. 327). Robert's conclusion drives directly to the core of the hospitality issue. Hospitality, if it is truly rooted in God's divine nature and forms the identity of the body of Christ, as we contend, must be at the forefront of mission and life for every church and every believer in some way, shape, or form. The "family of God" must bear witness to the world through hospitality. Since the "family of God" extends into the home of each believer, Robert concludes that "the first step [of recovery] is to restore the Christian home as a subject for the contextualized theory and practice of mission" (p. 327). To her conclusion, I would simply add that the home and the family are the foremost outposts for carrying out hospitality in the world.

As Charles Hoole further points out, in God's redemptive work "the church becomes a close-knit family of God" ("Redeeming the South Asian Family," *Transformation*, 19.1, 2002, p. 39). Touching the heart of American culture, Hoole observes that "the modern western notion of family as consisting of father, mother and children is somewhat alien to the Bible" (p. 39). Within the pages of the New Testament, for example, the notion of family or household would include extended family, close friends and perhaps even slaves, if any (cf. Acts 16:15, 31-34; 18:8). In light of this understanding of family, "new converts would certainly have been added to existing household communities" (p. 39). The *oikos* proved of vital importance for the life of the early church. As David J. Feddes similarly contends, "households were catalytic in the spread of early Christianity and formative in the structuring of its groups . . . the household was the key social unit for spreading Christianity" ("Caring for God's Household," *Calvin Theological Journal*, vol. 43, 2008, pp. 275-276). We have suggested that perhaps the reason hospitality and the "person of peace" concept seemingly work well within the Majority World may be due to the lack of the modern worldview. Feddes points in this direction when he states, "Such cultures bear more similarity to the New

Testament social context than does the contemporary West where a house tends to serve as strictly a private residence" (p. 277). As the "family of God" believers must embrace the stranger through hospitality which necessitates opening the private home to the "other" and subsequently making it public in order to play a role in transitioning the guest to "family." "As Jesus upholds family ties," writes Feddes, "he makes the household vital to his mission strategy and vision of transformed community" (p. 283).

In order for true and lasting transformational relationships to take root, genuine acceptance must be present. "It is within the family that we first experience ourselves being accepted and as accepting of others," writes Jose M. de Mesa, "as being affirmed and affirming as persons; it is where we experience mutual sharing, humbly receiving and generously giving" ("Re-Rooting Mission in the Family," *Mission Studies*, 19.1, 2002, p. 138). Through divine hospitality and God's generosity, believers are graciously admitted into a new family, the "family of God," and thus are given a new identity with new meaning and new purpose. Short-term hospitality, de Mesa notes, must grow into long-term familial relationships as the "family of God" because "family life is an authentic form of ecclesial life" (p. 149). And furthermore, "being family is being church" and "being family as church is being church in mission" (p. 149). To be the church of God is to be the family of God, and to be the family of God involves receiving and passing on the hospitality of God.

CHURCH FACILITIES AND HOSPITALITY

Lastly, we must also mention the role church facilities should play in hospitality. Church buildings need to have the same openness to the stranger and carry a family feel. Unfortunately, no home is equipped enough to house the size of many congregations. Church buildings do bring Christians together as the family of God; they must operate as one as well, which welcomes the stranger, seeing itself as host. Some ways in which churches have used their structures to demonstrate hospitality include, for example, outreach to immigrants, shelters for the homeless, and meeting space for the community, just to name a few. Churches need to re-think how to use their buildings and properties in a way that demonstrates the hospitality of God toward the surrounding community.

CHAPTER 6:

BRINGING THE CHURCH HOME

We set out at the beginning of this study to address three main items: (1) the western church being re-awakened to the mutual and reciprocal biblical definition of hospitality; (2) the need for the West to undergo some contextualization in order for the biblical role of hospitality and the "person of peace" to work in it; and (3) transitioning from short-term relational encounters of hospitality in the West, as indeed must happen in Africa and Asia as well, to long-term relationships as the "family of God."

In regard to defining hospitality biblically, we have noted several significant points. First, hospitality is rooted in the character of God himself. In creating the world, God was actually demonstrating hospitality toward humanity whom he created last. That humanity was the final act of creation suggests that it was invited into God's space, the Garden of Eden. In this space was relationship, identity, purpose, and abundance. Consequently, the Fall of Humanity appears as humanity's rejection of God's divine hospitality. The closed door to the Garden signified humanity's exit from God's space. Nonetheless, God's hospitality is constantly being manifested through his interactions with humanity over the course of history. God's interactions with the patriarchs as well as with Israel during the Wilderness Wanderings testify to this. God continually provides abundant hospitality to humanity in attempts to build deep, long-lasting relationship.

We also saw in the Old Testament humanity playing the role of host. We observed Abraham and Sarah, as well as Lot and his daughters utilize hospitality at important junctures with others. We also witnessed Abraham's servant as a recipient of hospitality from Rebekah and her family. Interestingly, in these instances we also witnessed the reciprocal nature of hospitality at work. Abraham shows hospitality to three visitors (two angels and God himself!) and as a result Abraham and Sarah are given the promise of a child which will fulfill God's promise given earlier to Abraham that he would be a "blessing to the nations." Lot entertained two strangers (two angels!) and the reciprocal result involved the physical salvation of Lot and his two daughters from the destruction of Sodom and Gomorrah. Abraham's servant utilized hospitality as a test in finding a wife for Isaac when he prayed to Yahweh asking him to send a woman who would respond favorably to his asking for a drink. This also resulted in moving a step closer toward the ultimate fulfillment of God's promise to Abraham to make him into a great nation. Humanity, as guest in its hospitable relationship with Yahweh, is also host to others, thus exemplifying the hospitality of God to the world and as such becoming an important personal means through which God is growing his kingdom.

We saw in the New Testament some similarities with the Old Testament portrait of hospitality, but we also saw some significant differences. One similarity involved the nature of hospitality itself. Hospitality was a means of carrying out God's greater purposes and mission in the world. We saw this in Paul's experiences with the islanders of Malta (Acts 28:1-10). Mutual hospitality resulted in Paul continuing his journey to Rome where he would boldly proclaim the gospel in the great city. Within the book of Acts, Paul's arrival at Rome fulfills Jesus' words in Acts 1:8 that his disciples will be witnesses of him "to the ends of the earth." The New Testament also showed hospitality as a defining characteristic of individual believers and churches as a whole. Closely related to this, hospitality as "entertaining strangers" involves welcoming both believers and non-believers, as the Synoptic "Missionary Discourse" of Jesus taught. Believers, as guests of God's abundant hospitality, are called to live a lifestyle demonstrating full reliance and trust in God's provision. Thus, for disciple-missionaries, they are to rely on the hospitality of other believers as they seek to carry out God's mission in the world. The "person of peace" according to these passages could be either an already existing believer in a given locale or a non-believer who is open to the gospel. Believers can be strangers to a Christian host as angels and Yahweh himself were to Abraham.

Furthermore, in connection to the ministry of Jesus Christ, he constantly lived a life that involved welcoming the "other." He ate with "sinners" and touched the untouchables in society, welcoming them into his presence and space, and thus into the presence and space of God himself. As a result, Christ-followers are called to welcome strangers and those on the fringes of society as a regular component of Christian living. Hospitality, welcoming the other, should be a defining characteristic of discipleship and the life of the church.

Secondly, the twin biblical components of hospitality and the "person of peace" have been put to good use in CPMs and CMMs throughout the Majority World with seemingly great success and explosive growth. One significant difference we noted between the biblical material and the modern material pertains to the definition of a "person of peace." According to the biblical witness, a "person of peace" could be either a believer or a non-believer. In contrast the modern material defines a "person of peace" as strictly a non-believer who is open to the gospel. In a related issue, we addressed the focus of rapid multiplication within Bruce Bennett's CPM model and several similar models. We noted that while this rapid and spontaneous growth has and does occur, it should not be fabricated by human ingenuity or mechanistic structures. Hospitality is risky and often uncertain. Its outcome cannot be controlled. As the Western church looks to contextualize the "person of peace" and hospitality we would do well to keep the influences of modernity ever before us. We must beware of forcing these missional concepts into a one-size-fits-all system. This will take time, effort and patience on behalf of Western Christians.

Finally, and perhaps the most significant component of our study, the western church must address the issue of relationships. Hospitality is short-term in nature and, as such, damage can occur to both guest and host if this short-term relationship is abused or ignored by either side. While hospitality is a key component to the ongoing mission of God, the church must seek to transition short-term hospitable encounters into lasting long-term relationships. I suggest that through hospitality the guest or stranger must transition into the church community, i.e., into the "family of God." As Stephen C. Barton contends, "Jesus' followers as his true family is augmented by the idea that followers are related to Jesus and to one another as 'brothers' [and 'sisters'], an idea intended to reinforce an ethic of humility and mutual acceptance" (*Discipleship and Family Ties*, p. 219). Hospitality essentially relies on humility and mutual acceptance on behalf of the guest and the host. In order for this to take place in the West, the western church must once again realize the vital role the house or household plays in the overall scheme of the Missio Dei. As a natural carryover, since the church is the "family of God" the hospitable use of church facilities must be a part of this discussion. It is unacceptable and poor stewardship to allow most church buildings to merely sit empty five or six days a week.

Hospitality played such a vital role in the life of the early church that Del Birkey "wonders if the first churches would have succeeded without their lavish attitude of hospitality" ("The House Church," *Missiology*, 19.1, January 1991, p. 94). Perhaps we could ask a similar question of the American church: In the midst of what appears to be an American church with decreasing influence, can the role of hospitality breathe new life into it? I believe it can if it makes the transition from short-term encounters to the long-term "family of God" relationships. The West must embrace hospitality as a "distinctly Christian principle of ministry" (Birkey, p. 94) and mission. We in the American church need to begin to see once again "houses as missional bases of operation" through which the role of hospitality becomes a defining hallmark (Roger W. Gehring, *House Church and Mission*, p. 227). It is within the home that both Christians and non-Christians can equally "experience the safety and security of the familia Dei" (Gehring, p. 293). The biblical title of "brother" and "sister" need to be embraced once again, at least in practice, and I believe hospitality can be a catalyst for this process.

Unfortunately, hospitality has been notably absent in the life of the American church. As Steve Atkerson asserts:

> It should arouse our suspicion of an underlying problem
> since this is one of the most blatantly disregarded mandates in

the modern church. Hospitality is practiced in a family setting. But if our families are being atomized into fragmented individuals, each with his own independent life to pursue, there is very little context for being hospitable (*House Church*, p. 172).

It is time for the American church, through the use of hospitality, to bring the church home. As Elizabeth Newman writes, "If the practice of hospitality is to flourish, the church needs to recover a more radical sense of home in the face of modern homelessness" (*Untamed Hospitality*, p. 51). Let the western church be reminded that "home" (*oikos*) is not necessarily located in a place, but rather "a people before God" (Newman, p. 51). Hospitality and home must be identified with the regular life of the church in America. Perhaps then we will witness new life breathed into a seemingly lifeless body and rapid growth of new believers added to it.

BIBLIOGRAPHY

COMMENTARIES:

Bruce, F. F. *The Book of the Acts: The New International Commentary of the New Testament*, rev. ed. (Eerdmans: Grand Rapids) 1988.

_____. *The Epistle to the Book of Hebrews: The New International Commentary on the New Testament*, rev. ed. (Eerdmans: Grand Rapids) 1990.

Cole, R. A. Mark: *Tyndale New Testament Commentary 2* (Eerdmans: Grand Rapids) 2002.

Danker, Frederick William, *A Greek-English Lexicon of the New Testament and Other Early Christian Literature*, 3rd ed. (Chicago: Chicago) 2000.

Dorsey, David A. *The Literary Structure of the Old Testament: A Commentary on Genesis – Malachi* (Grand Rapids: Baker) 1999.

Edwards, James R. *Romans: New International Biblical Commentary 6* (Peabody: Hendrickson) 1992.

Enns, Peter. *Exodus: The NIV Application Commentary* (Zondervan: Grand Rapids) 2000.

France, R. T. *The Gospel of Matthew: The New International Commentary on the New Testament* (Eerdmans: Grand Rapids) 2007.

_____. *The Gospel of Mark: The New International Greek Testament Commentary* (Eerdmans: Grand Rapids) 2002.

Guthrie, Donald. *The Pastoral Epistles: Tyndale New Testament Commentary 14* (Eerdmans: Grand Rapids) 2002.

Grudem, Wayne. *1 Peter: Tyndale New Testament Commentary 17* (Eerdmans: Grand Rapids) 2002.

Hagner, Donald A. *Hebrews: New International Biblical Commentary 14* (Peabody: Hendrickson) 1990.

Hamilton, Victor P. *The Book of Genesis, Chapters 1-17: The New International Commentary on the Old Testament* (Eerdmans: Grand Rapids) 1990.

_____. *The Book of Genesis, Chapters 18-50: The New International Commentary on the Old Testament* (Eerdmans: Grand Rapids) 1995.

Jacobsen, Thorkild. *The Treasures of Darkness: A History of Mesopotamian Religion* (New Haven: Yale University Press), 1976.

Keener, Craig S. *A Commentary on the Gospel of Matthew* (Eerdmans: Grand Rapids) 1999.

Knight III, George W. *The Pastoral Epistles: The New International Greek Testament Commentary* (Eerdmans: Grand Rapids) 1992.

Leifeld, Walter L. *Luke: The Expositor's Bible Commentary* (Grand Rapids: Zondervan) 1995.

Marshall, I. Howard. *Acts: Tyndale New Testament Commentary 5* (Eerdmans: Grand Rapids) 2002.

_____. *The Epistles of John: The New International Commentary on the New Testament.* (Eerdmans: Grand Rapids) 1978.

Moo, Douglas J. *The Epistle to the Romans: The New International Commentary on the New Testament* (Eerdmans: Grand Rapids) 1996.

Morris, Leon. *Luke: Tyndale New Testament Commentaries 3* (Grand Rapids: Eerdmans) 2002.

Stott, John R. W. *The Letters of John: Tyndale New Testament Commentary 19*. Eerdmans, Grand Rapids, 2002.

Walton, John H. *Genesis: The NIV Application Commentary* (Zondervan: Grand Rapids) 2001.

Wilson, Gerald H. *Psalms, vol. 1. The NIV Application Commentary* (Zondervan: Grand Rapids) 2002.

Witherington III, Ben. *Letters and Homilies for Hellenized Christians, vol. II: A Socio-Rhetorical Commentary on 1-2 Peter* (IVP: Downers Grove) 2007.

STUDIES:

Addison, Steve. *Movements That Change the World: Five Keys to Spreading the Gospel* (IVP: Downer's Grove) 2011.

Allen, Roland. *The Spontaneous Expansion of the Church* (Wipf and Stock: Eugene) 1962.

Atkerson, Steve, ed. *House Church: Simple, Strategic, Scriptural* (New Testament Restoration Fellowship: Atlanta) 2008.

Barton, Stephen C. *Discipleship and Family Ties in Mark and Matthew*. SNTSMS 80 (Cambridge: Cambridge) 1994.

Beale, Greg. *The Temple and the Church's Mission: A biblical theology of the dwelling place of God: New Studies in Biblical Theology 17* (IVP: Downers Grove) 2004.

Bennett, Bruce. *Community Church Planting Manual*. Unpublished. Available at www.intoafricaproject.org.

Bonk, Jonathan J. *Missions and Money: Affluence as a Missionary Problem Revisited*, revised and expanded ed. (Orbis: Maryknoll) 2006.

Buckwalter, H. Douglas. *The Character and Purpose of Luke's Christology*, SNTSMS 89 (Cambridge: Cambridge) 1996.

Carroll R., M. Daniel. *Christians at the Border: Immigration, the Church and the Bible* (Baker: Grand Rapids) 2008.

Donovan, Vincent. *Christianity Rediscovered* (Orbis: Maryknoll) 1978.

Garrison, David. *Church Planting Movements: How God is Redeeming a Lost World* (WIGTake Resources: Arkadelphia) 2004.

Gehring, Roger W. *House Church and Mission: The Importance of Household Structures in Early Christianty* (Peabody: Hendrickson) 2004.

Haile, Ahmed Ali. *Teatime in Mogadishu: My Journey as a Peace Ambassador in the World of Islam* (Herald: Harrisonburg) 2011.

Heuretz, Christopher L., and Christine D. Pohl. *Friendship at the Margins: Discovering Mutuality in Service and Mission* (IVP: Downers Grove) 2010.

Hiebert, Paul G. *Transforming Worldviews: An Anthropological Understanding of How People Change* (Baker: Grand Rapids) 2008.

Kaylor, R. David. *Paul's Covenant Community: Jews & Gentiles in Romans* (John Knox: Atlanta) 1988.

Knight, Douglas H. *The Eschatological Economy: Time and the Hospitality of God* (Eerdmans: Grand Rapids) 2006.

Koenig, John. *New Testament Hospitality: Partnership with Strangers as Promise and Mission* (Fortress: Philadelphia) 1985.

Newman, Elizabeth. *Untamed Hospitality: Welcoming God and Other Strangers* (Brazos: Grand Rapids) 2007.

Oden, Amy, ed. *And You Welcomed Me: A Sourcebook on Hospitality in Early Christianity* (Abingdon: Nashville) 2001.

Ogletree, Thomas W. *Hospitality to the Stranger: Dimensions of Moral Understanding* (Fortress: Philadelphia) 1985.

Palmer, Parker J. *The Company of Strangers: Christians and the Renewal of America's Public Life* (Crossroad Publishing: New York) 1983.

Platt, David. *Radical: Taking Back Your Faith from the American Dream* (Colorado Springs: Multnomah) 2010.

Pohl, Christine D. *Making Room: Recovering Hospitality as a Christian Tradition* (Eerdmans: Grand Rapids) 1999.

Rah, Soong-Chan. *The Next Evangelicalism: Freeing the Church from Western Cultural Captivity* (IVP: Downers Grove) 2009.

Smith, Steve, and Ying Kai. *T4T: A Discipleship Re-Revolution* (WIGTake: Arkadelphia) 2001.

Walls, Andrew F. *The Missionary Movement in Christian History: Studies in the Transmission of the Faith* (Orbis: Maryknoll) 1996.

Wan, Enoch, ed. *Diaspora Missiology: Theory, Methodology, and Practice* (Institute of Diaspora Studies – USA @ Western Seminary: Eugene) 2011.

Volf, Miroslav. *Exclusion and Embrace: A Theological Exploration of Identity, Otherness, and Reconciliation* (Abingdon: Nashville) 1996.

Yong, Amos. *Hospitality & the Other: Pentecost, Christian Practices, and the Neighbor* (Orbis: Maryknoll) 2008.

ARTICLES:

Barton, Stephen C. "Living as Families in the Light of the New Testament." *Interpretation*, vol. 52 no 2, November-December 2000, pp. 130-144.

Beare, F. W. "The Mission of the Disciples and the Mission Charge: Matthew 10 and Parallels." *Journal of Biblical Literature*, vol. 89, 1970, pp. 1-13.

Birkey, Del. "The House Church: A Missiological Model." *Missiology*, vol. 19 no. 1, January 1991, pp. 69-80.

Bonk, Jonathan. "Thinking Small: Toward a Missiology of Interruption." *McClure Lectures, Pittsburg Theological Seminary, September 27-28, 2010*, pp. 1-17.

Booser, Kimberly D. "The Literary Structure of John 1:1-18: An Examination of Its Theological Implications Concerning God's Saving Plan through Jesus Christ." *Evangelical Journal* 16 (Spring 1998) pp.

de Mesa, Jose M. "Re-rooting Mission in the Family." *Mission Studies*, vol. 19 no 1, 2002, pp. 137-54.

Faircloth, Kyle. "Searching for the Indigenous Method." *Evangelical Missions Quarterly*, vol. 48 no. 4, October 2012, pp. 396-402.

Feddes, David J. "Caring for God's Household: A Leadership Paradigm among New Testament Christians and Its Relevance for Church and Mission Today." *Calvin Theological Journal*, no. 43, 2008, pp. 274-99.

Gittins, Anthony J. "Beyond Hospitality? The Missionary Status and Role Revisited." *Currents in Theology and Mission*, vol. 21 no 3, June 1994, pp.

Hoole, Charles. "Redeeming the South Asian Family: Mission as Extending the Household of God." *Transformation*, vol. 19 no 1, January 2002, pp. 37-41.

Koyama, Kosuke. "Extend Hospitality to Strangers." *International Review of Mission*, vol. 82 no 327, July-October 1993, pp.

Malina, Bruce J. "The Received Text and What it Cannot Do: III John and Hospitality." *Semeia* 35, 1986, pp. 171-94.

Morschauser, Scott. "'Hospitality,' Hostiles and Hostages: On the Legal Background to Genesis 19:1-9." *Journal for the Study of the Old Testament*, vol. 27 no 4, June 2003, pp. 461-85.

Pohl, Christine D. "Biblical Issues in Mission and Migration." *Missiology: An International Review*, vol. 31 no 1, January 2003. pp. 3-15.

Robert, Dana L. "What Happened to the Christian Home? The Missing Component of Mission Theory." *Missiology: An International Review*, vol. 33 no 3, July 2005, pp. 325-40.

Rogers, T. J. "Shaking the Dust off the Markan Mission Discourse." *Journal for the Study of the New Testament*, vol. 27 no 2 2004. pp. 169-92.

Stetzer, Ed. "The State of the Church in America: Hint: It's Not Dying. *The Exchange* [Blog]. http://www.christianitytoday.com/edstetzer/2013/october/state-of-american-church.html. Last accessed 10/30/2014.

Vogels, Walter. "Hospitality in Biblical Perspective." *Liturgical Ministry*, vol. 11. Fall 2002, pp. 161-73.

Yamauchi, Edwin. "Jesus Outside the New Testament: What is the Evidence?" in *Jesus Under Fire: Modern Scholarship Reinvents the Historical Jesus*, ed. Michael J. Wilkins and J. P. Moreland, pp. 207-30 (Zondervan: Grand Rapids) 1995.

ALSO FROM ENERGION PUBLICATIONS

The Jesus Paradigm

David Alan Black

Black writes an immensely practical book that will rearrange the furniture in your mind and, if heeded, will resurrect biblical Christianity.

David B. Capes
Professor in Christianity, Houston
Baptist University

COMING SPRING, 2015
IN THE
TOPICAL LINE DRIVES SERIES

A Cup of Cold Water
Dr. Chris Surber

Putting the Gospel into action!

MORE FROM ENERGION PUBLICATIONS

Personal Study
Holy Smoke! Unholy Fire	Bob McKibben	$14.99
The Jesus Paradigm	David Alan Black	$17.99
When People Speak for God	Henry Neufeld	$17.99
The Sacred Journey	Chris Surber	$11.99

Christian Living
It's All Greek to Me	David Alan Black	$3.99
Grief: Finding the Candle of Light	Jody Neufeld	$8.99
My Life Story	Becky Lynn Black	$14.99
Crossing the Street	Robert LaRochelle	$16.99
Life as Pilgrimage	David Moffett-Moore	14.99

Bible Study
Learning and Living Scripture	Lentz/Neufeld	$12.99
From Inspiration to Understanding	Edward W. H. Vick	$24.99
Philippians: A Participatory Study Guide	Bruce Epperly	$9.99
Ephesians: A Participatory Study Guide	Robert D. Cornwall	$9.99
Ecclesiastes: A Participatory Study Guide	Russell Meek	$9.99

Theology
Creation in Scripture	Herold Weiss	$12.99
Creation: the Christian Doctrine	Edward W. H. Vick	$12.99
The Politics of Witness	Allan R. Bevere	$9.99
Ultimate Allegiance	Robert D. Cornwall	$9.99
History and Christian Faith	Edward W. H. Vick	$9.99
The Journey to the Undiscovered Country	William Powell Tuck	$9.99
Process Theology	Bruce G. Epperly	$4.99

Ministry
Clergy Table Talk	Kent Ira Groff	$9.99
Out of This World	Darren McClellan	$24.99

Generous Quantity Discounts Available
Dealer Inquiries Welcome
Energion Publications — P.O. Box 841
Gonzalez, FL_ 32560
Website: http://energionpubs.com
Phone: (850) 525-3916

www.ingramcontent.com/pod-product-compliance
Lightning Source LLC
Chambersburg PA
CBHW051845040426
42447CB00006B/701